DONALD MORRISON'S MEGANTIC COUNTRY

QUEBEC, CANADA

Scale 1" : 4½ m.

0   2   4   m

Winslow

Felton River

noway

Whitton (township)

Chaudière River

uisla emetery

Whitton Lake

Spring Hill

John Boston's Corner

Carpenter's camp

MARSDEN

Ayres' Sugarbush

DRUMAVACH Echo Vale ROAD

Disputed farm on Ness Hill

MEGANTIC

Christie MacArthur's

Echo Vale Cemetery

Sandy Bay

Agnes

Marsboro

Lake Megantic

Piopolis

MOUNTAIN

WANTED:
DONALD MORRISON

Books by Clarke Wallace

MONTREAL ADVENTURE
THE COMPLETE SNOWMOBILER

WANTED: DONALD MORRISON

THE TRUE STORY
OF THE MEGANTIC OUTLAW

BY CLARKE WALLACE

Doubleday Canada Limited, Toronto, Ontario
Doubleday & Company, Inc., Garden City, New York
1977

Library of Congress Cataloging in Publication Data

Wallace, Clarke.
 Wanted—Donald Morrison: the true story of the Megantic outlaw.

 1. Morrison, Donald. 2. Crime and criminals—Québec (Province)—
Biography. I. Title.
HV6248.M774W34   364.1'525'0924 [B]
ISBN: 0-385-12647-6
Library of Congress Catalog Card Number 76-42409

To my wife, Stephanie,
and my friend
J. Robert Morrison.
He started it all;
she kept it going.

CONTENTS

CONTENTS

AUTHOR'S NOTE

In the first half of the nineteenth century hundreds of thousands of Scottish clansmen turned their backs on the oppression about them and sought a new life abroad. Some traveled no further than the European mainland while others struck out for such distant colonies as New Zealand, Australia, the United States—and Canada.

Many were to find their new land no less oppressive and move on. Most remained, realizing that no matter where they went, life would never be a hoped-for bed of roses.

Such were Murdo and Sophia Morrison, who left their barren Hebrides island of Lewis off the Scottish coast in 1838 and came to Canada to settle in the Eastern Townships of Quebec. The youngest among their five sons, whom they named Donald, became known as the "Megantic Outlaw." This is the story of Donald Morrison, who stood up in protest against an old evil—those ruthless persons who, acting within the law of a sophisticated society, sought to confiscate a man's homestead and birthright.

The events recorded here are true. *No* names have been changed. A fictional approach has been used only in the hope of bringing alive the hardships, joys, and tragedies which faced unwary immigrants and to portray better one man's struggle to live by the code "to thine own self be true."

Any conversation quoted, however, has been taken directly from personal accounts, newspaper files, or court records.

If a man does not keep pace with his companions, perhaps it is because he hears a different drummer. Let him step to the music which he hears, however measured or far away.

HENRY DAVID THOREAU

ONE

HOMECOMING

1

EASTWARD HO!

SEPTEMBER 1883

Donald Morrison sighed as he loosened the well-worn girth and slid the saddle effortlessly off the gelding's back. Selling that saddle would be the hardest. For seven years it had been part of him, and though horses had come and gone, and friends too, for that matter, his Texas saddle had stuck with him. He'd stitched and patched and saddle soaped it in lonely bunkhouses and beside grub wagons from the Saskatchewan to the Rio Grande and it was still in good shape. But there'd be little point in dragging it back with him, for he'd have no use for a cowboy saddle in the Eastern Townships of Quebec. Or for his guns either. Just the same, he would keep his Colts, as souvenirs of wilder days.

As he reached down absently to put the saddle by his feet, his arm brushed against his vest pocket and he heard paper crinkle. That would be the letter. The letter, soiled, wrinkled, and travel-stained, that had finally caught up to him at a camp near Choteau in Montana Territory, and had brought him across the rolling cattle country and northward over the bordering Rockies with their jagged, sawed-off peaks and narrow, twisting valleys. Then he had dropped down into the sun-parched grasslands of the foothills and Indian country, heading north by northwest.

He came upon something the fourth day. At first it looked nothing more than a lump on the horizon. As he came closer, squinting into the morning sun, he heard first the faint staccato of hammers and watched as the lump separated itself into two distinct shapes. One was a flatcar piled high with steel rails and beside it, with his rifle at the easy, was a member of the North-west Mounted Police, unmounted, his pillbox hat set at a jaunty angle and his ammunition belt, studded with cartridges, cinched tight about his waist.

Morrison stopped, nodded, and leaned an arm across the pommel. His eyes dropped to the twin rails and he followed them eastward as they narrowed, became one, and blurred from sight. His eyes swung back. These same rails went no further than a few inches beyond the solid iron wheels of the flatcar. From here an orderly file of square-cut wood ties carried on westward with such uniformity and precision that it seemed a sergeant major must have drilled them into such a tidy forma-tion.

A quarter of a mile farther on these ties dropped into a small coulee from which rose the sounds of construction. Standing in his stirrups the cowboy could make out the forms of men stoop-ing and digging and hammering as they set the ties securely in the freshly leveled ground. The racket they made floated back on the crisp morning air announcing to the empty spaces that the Canadian Pacific Railway was coming through.

Morrison was amazed that the railway had reached this far, for when he had come West seven years ago, in 1876, the pro-posed east-west rail line had been bogged down east of Win-nipeg. It was a moot question whether the scheme was mired deeper in political red tape or in the unstable muskeg around Rat Portage and Cross River. Either was capable of swallowing an entire railway system, but this linking of the country from sea to sea was the price of confederation, and now the Canadian Pacific was heading hell bent for British Columbia, if it could find its way through the Rockies.

The Mountie was glad to see him. Keeping an eye on a flatcar and its contents wasn't the Mountie's happiest assignment and even the briefest companionship was a welcome relief.

They talked, and the Mountie told him he could catch an eastbound train from Calgary, since service had begun there a month before. He'd have no trouble finding Calgary, the policeman said, just follow the tracks. Morrison had grinned. Though he could find his way anywhere, day or night, tracks or no tracks, his route north had brought him a little too far west; too close to the mountains. He nodded and pulled the reins gently across the horse's neck, turning him east. He didn't look back.

The station was pandemonium. Trainmen, panicked by the newness of the whole thing, plunged aimlessly back and forth over the bright, new wood platform shouting orders and "All aboards," only to have them go unnoticed in the general confusion.

Even the disgruntled snorts from the Countess of Dufferin, the Canadian Pacific's first proud locomotive (named after a former Governor-General's beautiful dark-haired wife) were lost in the turmoil as she stood before the temporary platform. Half an hour late she was, and judging from the unabating chaos, she might never turn her wheels again.

About her jammed sweat-soaked miners, weathered cowboys, and laughing, shrieking children tethered at arms' length to anxious mothers who eyed the Countess from a safe distance. Over the platform scurried the businessmen and shopkeepers of the frontier town, bent on retrieving mailings and goods expected weeks earlier, only to find they would have to wait for the next delivery, or possibly the one after that. Here too were the rustlers and homesteaders and the ladies and the not-so-ladies of the pioneer community rubbing shoulders and bumping elbows with frazzled clerks and weary, slumped-shouldered immigrants, those wide-eyed wanderers who stood, jostled and stunned, unable to comprehend that *this*, at last, was the end of the rainbow.

Somewhat detached from the hubbub below, Donald Morrison sat alone in the train's colonist coach, four wagons back from the restless Countess. The train's delay had suited the cowboy, giving him enough time to do what had to be done but not enough to brood over the transactions. Selling the saddle *had* been difficult, and parting with his gelding hadn't been easy either. It was too much like saying good-by to his old way of life. But he'd got a good price for them, enough for him to purchase a single-fare ticket East without having to dig into his money belt.

Ensuring that he had forgotten nothing, Morrison glanced beneath him. The suitcase, claimed earlier at the stagecoach depot, was in place, along with his bedroll, and as he shifted his spare, hardened body along the slatted wood seat, seeking some modicum of comfort, he let his eyes wander over the scene below and beyond the coach window. The crowd was surging back and forth along the platform, reminding him of prairie grass caught in a ripple of wind.

He watched for a moment, then sighed and stretched as his hand came unconsciously up to touch the money belt under his rough cotton shirt. Yes, still there. And the money he had counted again at dawn would still be there too. Nearly $2,000, even though he had sent regular payments home each year. Two thousand dollars. Seven years of cattle driving, all over the continent, beginning as a tenderfoot cowboy in the drag of a drive where the dust from the bawling cattle filled the eyes and drove its way through the bandanna which covered mouth and nose, as though it weren't there. He had worked hard, learned fast, and soon progressed from riding night herd, to circle and finally to point. For seven years he'd weathered everything; Texas dust storms, icy swollen waters in Colorado, coaxing his mount back to the bunkhouse in Montana blizzards, tracking across the parched lands south of the Saskatchewan, or sucking in all the breath he could muster as he and his horse battled for footing high in the Rockies.

Yes, he had been through just about everything trail bosses and the weather could throw at him, and he'd come through in one piece, age twenty-five, healthy as a mule—and $2,000 richer. This modest fortune would stem the family plight in Megantic.

Megantic. He could see the road which galloped down from the farm on Ness Hill to Megantic village below, the bluish-green waters of Lake Megantic stretching out from the tree-lined shore as it eased itself around a wide bend heading toward Sandy Bay and Piopolis. He didn't have to close his eyes to imagine the Megantic railroad station, the Prince of Wales Hotel, the American House—or Pope's, as it was called informally—where the lake narrowed and grudgingly forced itself within the confines of the neck of the Chaudière River. He used to think a lot about Megantic when he first came West, but memories faded like old parchment as new ones took their place.

Then the letter came. As he read it and reread it many times, Megantic seemed like yesterday. They wanted him home. He sensed the urgency between the lines. His father would never plead, but it too was there, buried deep in the Gaelic. Something was obviously wrong; it was time to go home. As he had headed north to meet the new railroad, he'd remained long enough in Dupuyer, Montana Territory, to post a letter to his parents telling them of his plans, although in the back of his mind he wondered why, being the youngest, his presence was so important. Maybe because it had been agreed that when they became too old to cope with the farm, Donald would take it over. Still, it didn't make sense, with his brothers and sisters so close . . . !

Suddenly the blast of an angry train whistle brought him half out of his seat. Up front the Countess, anxious to get underway, fumed and snorted as she worked up a good head of steam. Finally, after more whistles and shouts from the surrounding crowd, the large, steel, driving wheels of the engine began to move.

Back in that colonist coach, one of four to make up the train, Donald Morrison settled back once more against the hard seat, looking around at the less than half a dozen who would share with him the long trip back East. The journey home to Megantic would be long and tedious. About as long a trip as his parents had made from Scotland to the Eastern Townships of Quebec forty-five years earlier, when his father, Murdo Morrison, had been just Donald's age, or a year older.

2

LOOKING BACK

SEPTEMBER 1883

By morning the smell of coal oil from the single overhead brass lamp had permeated the entire coach. Morrison, having spent the night in one of the berths, which were hinged to the wall above the seats and lowered by chains to a horizontal position, found sleep only something less unbearable than it would have been sitting upright in the seat below. The thin cotton ticking supplied as a mattress left much to be desired; his bedroll had taken some of the discomfort out of it. He preferred the ground and open sky.

He had arisen early and now, slumped in the seat, he worked his tongue across his dry lips, tasting the pungent essence of the kerosene. Suddenly the corners of his mouth softened. Maybe he should have planned a more peaceful ride home—on horseback. Then he sighed, shifted in the seat, and watched the rolling countryside slowly flatten itself into humorless prairie—Moose Jaw, Indian Head, Flat Creek. With the miles clack-clacking beneath him, his thoughts drifted back to his parents and their journey to eastern Canada back in 1838. He'd heard the story years ago, told in Gaelic, at his mother's knee, and he still remembered every last detail. . . .

The sheep had come in droves, spreading like a disease first across the Highlands of Scotland, then north to the Orkneys, and finally west to the Hebrides. But sheep were not the only enemy. The English had beaten the clans at Culloden in 1745, and since then the great families had not been as strong. On top of that, generations of Scottish fathers had divided the land among their sons until the countryside was dotted with portions of property barely large enough to survive on, let alone divide again. To the crofter or farmer, the Highland animals, mainly black cattle and sheep, though thin and scrawny creatures from lack of good grazing land, provided life-giving milk and wool. They were too valuable to eat and indeed became so much a part of the family that each, at birth, was given a name. At this time "sheep country" was confined to the southern part, or Lowlands of Scotland where winter was less severe. Then, around 1760, a farmer in the Cheviot Hills bred a sheep which was hardier, woolier, and took to winter like a snowshoe rabbit. These "Cheviots" could survive and grow fat where even the black cattle had trouble scratching a meal from the barren Highlands. Soon the crofters, who owned no land of their own, found themselves shunted aside to make room for these profitable sheep. And they were forced to move on.

The Hebrides, the string of rocky islands off the rugged west coast of Scotland, were the last to feel the shockwave of invading Cheviots. For hundreds of years families like the MacNeils, MacLeods, Morrisons, MacAulays, and MacDonalds had lived there as crofters. Now their rented patches of farmland became pastures as they were pushed out to fend for themselves. And that, for many, meant going to Canada.

To Donald Morrison the stories of the suffering endured by the Scottish settlers on their way to the New World lingered like a bad dream. As a boy his imagination was set afire by tales of rotting ships, crammed to the gunwales with the sick, passengers dying from cholera, dysentery, or typhus; of sea captains who refused to break open fresh supplies of food because feeding the destitute was not part of their contracts. Such stories had a profound effect on Donald, for this would be his first taste of man's inhumanity to his fellow man, and as he grew older he recognized it all around him. The worst was hearing how his very own family had suffered in the same way. He remembered his mother telling him how they too had wanted to leave the Isle of Lewis.

His mother, Sophia MacKenzie, was born in Barvas near the northwest coast of the island on May 24, 1818. At age eighteen she married Murdoch "Murdo" Morrison, a man five years her senior, who had come from neighboring Valtas. They had been married two years when they realized that, unless a person had money to invest in sheep, life at home held little promise. But where could they go? They thought of the colonies, dismissing Australia and New Zealand as being too far. Like so many others, they settled for Canada. Somewhere during the arrangements, through the British American Land Company, they decided to make the Eastern Townships of Lower Canada their new home. Thus, on a wet day in midsummer 1838, they packed their meager belongings and clutching their worldly wealth, set out for the port of Stornoway on the east side of Lewis.

When they arrived they learned that their ship would not sail for Canada until the passenger list was complete. How long would it take, they asked, knowing full well their money wouldn't last long in Stornoway. A week, a month, a shipping official said. Later, talking to others in the same predicament, they found it to be true. Some ships hadn't sailed for months, leaving would-be passengers at the mercy of unscrupulous boardinghouse proprietors, who charged exorbitant prices, knowing the emigrants were forced to wait from day to day for passage.

And day by day the Morrisons grew more discouraged as they saw their savings dwindle. They had been in Stornoway a week, determined to hold on, when news came that their ship would sail in two days. They were overjoyed. Arriving early at the dock they found their ship was much smaller than they expected. It was sea-stained and battered and in places the timbers were so rotten that bits could be picked away with the fingers. But they couldn't be fussy; they climbed eagerly aboard with their possessions.

Conditions were appalling. Passengers already had been stuffed in everywhere like cattle, and Sophia and Murdo were left to fend for themselves to find room in corridors, on floors, anywhere. Many of the would-be settlers, arriving after the Morrisons, were jammed deep down in the damp, dark, rat-filled holds where they served as human ballast. Here disease ran rampant; food was either scarce or putrid. Somehow Sophia and

Murdo survived, bolstered by a handful of newly found friends who banded together, encouraging each other to hold on until the journey finally ended at the Port of Quebec.

Memories of his mother's stories flooded Donald Morrison's mind as he watched the Canadian prairie pass by the window of the train that was carrying him home.

The letter from Donald, which arrived Friday, put Sophia Morrison into a spin. She had fully expected Donald to say no. It was so far, she had thought, and as with so many others who had gone West (like another son Malcolm and his wife), he would never come back. Then on Friday, September 28, at the Echo Vale station, Mr. Jones handed her a letter postmarked, Dupuyer, Montana Territory, September 15, 1883. She stood stock still staring at the bluish two-cent stamp with a profile of George Washington etched on it.

Excited beyond belief, Sophia rushed out of the station and was halfway up the Tenth Range Road before she stopped to tear the envelope open. She didn't want to read it. Maybe he'd say he was sorry but . . . ! Her hands trembled as she hastily extracted the paper inside and unfolded it. Her eyes darted across the words without reading them. The message was short and in Gaelic. Bad Gaelic. Wrong tenses. *Wrong* tenses. And misspellings. Good heavens, the boy was going to pieces. Shaking uncontrollably, she forced her eyes from one word to the other, seeking out meanings. He was well, he was . . . on his way home. Sophia Morrison's wrinkled hands stopped shaking. She looked up at the blue sky and slowly closed her eyes; he hadn't let them down. And she cried.

Today, Tuesday, October 2, Sophia Morrison sat in the high-backed chair looking about her. The small, modest home on Ness Hill was spotless. And it should be, for every day now she had set about cleaning it after Murdo had gone out to do the chores. Every day she wiped and cleaned and scrubbed because she had to do something to keep her mind occupied. The thought of waiting even a few more days was almost unbearable.

Her Donald. He had been a tall, strapping boy when he left seven years before, his strong physique formed by years spent wrestling with tree stumps and rocks as he helped his father clear the land and push back the forest. He had been just eighteen when he told them he was going West with his friend Norman MacAulay. She remembered how she fought back the tears on seeing the quiet eagerness in his face. She had seen the same look on Murdo's face when they had told their families on Lewis that they were leaving the Hebrides for Canada.

Sophia sighed and let her hands drop onto her lap. She wore a simple cotton dress, which until now had always been reserved for Sundays. This was the fifth day in a row she had put it on after lunch and was half afraid she'd wear it out before Donald finally arrived. It had worn well over the years, she thought as she looked at her nut-brown hardened hands. She had worn well too, come to think of it, though sometimes she wondered how she had ever done so. What amazed her most, these days in particular, was that somehow she had reached her sixty-fifth year. What ever happened to her fifties, for goodness' sake? The last time she thought of age was on her *forty-fifth* birthday—and even that seemed ancient at the time. Praise heaven though, she still had her health. She was a smallish woman—less to take care of, her mother had always said—though now she was given to roundness and her soft brown hair had become crinkly gray.

The hardships of pioneer life showed visibly on Sophia's hands and face, its smoothness broken here and there by deep wrinkles. But this face told more than hardships. It showed that its owner had met life square on with no regrets, no misgivings. Well, not many. Coming to Canada had been torturous, but she had never regretted it.

Even now, the humiliation of that thirteen-week Atlantic crossing lingered. There had been times during the voyage that she had thought neither she nor Murdo would reach Canada alive. A tragic number of passengers aboard hadn't; the Morrisons counted themselves among the lucky ones. Arriving in their newly adopted country, they both tried to put the past behind them when, with a few friends they had met aboard the ship, they rounded up their belongings and sought some transportation south to their new holdings.

In the years to come Sophia would relive the terrible hundred-mile journey overland to Sherbrooke, and thence to Red

Mountain and Lingwick, through stories she recounted to her children and grandchildren. "Transportation" for Sophia, Murdo, and a dozen others they had become friendly with on the ship was nothing more than a small, broken cart and a weary horse bought at an outrageous price. It carried some of their possessions and children too small to walk. Unknowingly they set out from Quebec into the eye of a nightmare.

Many times they lost the trail and had to make their own as they bumped and fought their way over hills and rocks and streams. At night the temperature plunged to freezing as it bit savagely through their loose clothing. Then came freezing rain which continued endlessly for days, soaking them to the skin. And yet they pressed on, even when provisions ran low and there was barely enough to feed the children. Stopping at scattered settlements, the settlers, almost as poor as the travelers, gave them more than they could spare—and wished them well.

Hills and mountains that seemed insurmountable were scaled; rivers that seemed too deep were forded. And when the bedraggled party finally stumbled into Sherbrooke four weeks later tragedy struck once more, with the death of Mrs. Donald MacIver, a woman who had been an added source of strength during the voyage and subsequent overland trek. Weakened and sick from the month-long ordeal, she had collapsed and died in her husband's arms as they reached the outskirts of the small town.

Struck dumb by the suddenness of her death (his wife had hidden the pain of her suffering), the distraught MacIver wandered the rain-soaked streets, blaming himself for having brought her to a country which in such a short time had given her so much grief. The other members of the party were equally shocked. Ever since they had left the Hebrides, the hardships they had all suffered had drawn them together. They shared MacIver's stunning sense of loss.

Leaving their horse and dumpcart at Arm's boardinghouse, Sophia, Murdo, and the others were directed up a dirt street past Loomis' bakery and Otis King's tavern. They found the British American Land Company office to be an unpretentious, low-structured building with a wide brick veranda. Stepping through the door in utter silence and grief, they were met by a well-dressed, intense young man named Peter McGill, who informed them, after introductions were made, that each family could have from fifty to one hundred acres of land. Then he smiled, almost paternally. The hundred-acre lots would be the more profitable, he ventured. The price was $3.00 an acre, one fifth payable immediately in cash, the remainder in five yearly installments.

Sophia could remember the silence that followed his remarks. She remembered the feeling of frustration building up within her as the young man glanced, smiling one to the other. Surely the land was free, she thought to herself as she fought down her emotions. Three dollars an acre was sheer robbery.

With little money between them, negotiations began. When the necessary papers were signed, McGill issued each family a rough-sketched map of the company's St. Francis territory holdings located well east of Sherbrooke. He pointed out the small settlements of Gould, North Hill, and Red Mountain in the Lingwick area. Each family had settled for a hundred-acre parcel of land. With it came enough oatmeal to last each family over the coming winter, because they had missed the planting season, McGill added gratuitously. And what did he ask in return, Murdo Morrison had asked? McGill shrugged. Little, he said, only that the men would be expected to grub out roads in the area in the spring. The next day the small party began their thirty-eight-mile trek back into the dense forests on only a slightly less hazardous route than the one from Quebec, with the pine box bearing Mrs. MacIver's body loaded aboard the small cart. It had been her last request to be buried at the new homestead.

Two days later the weary travelers reached Lingwick. The view of the rolling hills and low mountains breaking the horizon filled them with hope. They shook hands here, catching their emotions before these got the best of them, and each family went in search of its land.

Sophia and Murdo headed three miles farther north, then bore slightly east until they found themselves atop Red Mountain. Here at last was their new home. And here Sophia discovered her greatest fears were realized: it wasn't land they had purchased, but rather impenetrable forest.

Selkirk, Whitemouth, Keewatin. By three o'clock Sunday morning, September 23, Morrison was still awake, his head rumbling with the incessant clatter of the carriage, broken only by the occasional blast of the train's whistle as it acknowledged the tiny settlements it passed. Hawk Lake, Eagle River. Dawn found the train between Wabigoon and Bonheur, but a thick, unfriendly autumn haze reduced the countryside to ten yards of bush on either side of the tracks.

Others in the coach had once again turned to railroad euchre and less thoughtful games while Morrison found himself in a quandary of emotions. His boyhood friend Norman MacAulay, whom he'd come West with, had tried to convince him his "home" was no longer back East but rather where, eventually, dreams of having their own spreads one day *would* come true. The whole country was moving West, Canada was growing fast, and the future would be here. He knew Norman was right—but the letter from his father had changed their plans.

English River, Savanne, Poland Swamp, Fort William, Prince Arthur's Landing. He'd miss Norman MacAulay, for they had been a good team, even though their approaches to life had been quite different. MacAulay was a whimsical fellow, who treated life as it came with a grin or shrug, but Morrison took a far more serious approach to it. Indeed, Morrison's aim in making the trip West, at least in part, was to send money back to pay off the family mortgage back East; MacAulay spent his money as it came.

New to the life in the West, both had thrown themselves into any sort of jobs, Morrison always being the one to explain carefully he'd never done this work before but was willing to try, while MacAulay would say he'd done it before a thousand times, but needed a little practice to "get the kinks out" because it was some time since he'd tackled that sort of work. The latter would often laugh uproariously at Morrison's cautious approach to everything. In turn Morrison couldn't help but admire MacAulay's bravado in handling every new situation with a verve which, often as not, got them in and out of things they might not otherwise have tackled. It had been a good combination, MacAulay's wild schemes being tempered by Morrison's fervent desire to stay alive.

Staying alive wasn't all that easy, they learned rather speedily. The American West was a lawless country. Life was measured on a day-to-day basis, something which came easy to MacAulay but was a hard lesson for Morrison. Living to the end of the day became an individual credo. They hardened fast, finding early that their deeply traditioned Presbyterian backgrounds took second place to the awful need to learn the use of guns for self-protection. After months and months of practice, both could handle revolvers and rifles with equal facility; it was obvious they were playing a grim game of survival of the fittest. To ensure they remained among "the fittest" each wore Colt .38 revolvers.

Countless times they had ridden to Texas to join cattle drives which were heading back north to meet government contracts for beef. Together they spent days and nights seldom out of the saddle, moving across badlands and over mountains, driving cattle northward only to be stopped by wary bands of Indians or surrounded at watering holes by the crudest, dirtiest, vilest of hombres who demanded "tax" per steer for the privilege of taking water from a source that belonged to no one. Bandits, rustlers, they had met them all. Men who would come out of the night to stampede their herds and in the melee of bawling cattle and neighing horses steal away a hundred or two, only to hold them for ransom until the man in charge bought them back at so much a head. Yes, it had been a wild, crazy life, and together they had roamed about, happily living for themselves. And then the letter came.

Morrison had hoped that MacAulay might come back East with him, but his friend merely passed it off with the wave of his hand. He'd likely finish this present drive then hit Texas again, tickling a few more female fannies along the way.

Parting hadn't been easy. MacAulay gave his friend the familiar half smile, the head cocked a little to the right, the lazy roll of his shoulders as he brought his hand up to shake Morrison's. For an instant Morrison thought his friend might change his mind, but the other just wished him Godspeed and turned away.

Morrison and the Countess parted at Prince Arthur's Landing. From there a steamship bore him across Lake Superior and down into Lake Huron and Georgian Bay to the port of Owen Sound and the waiting train of the Toronto Grey and Bruce Railway line.

Toronto, Kingston, Montreal, and at last the familiar outlines of the high, humped-back Sherbrooke station straddling the tracks down by the St. Francis River. It was Tuesday, October 2.

With time on his hands before the 3:45 P.M. train left for Megantic, Morrison wandered about the town of five thousand inhabitants which he had visited many times in the past. But his mind was preoccupied with what he'd find later that afternoon. Of the seven children born to Murdo and Sophia Morrison only Malcolm, the eldest son, would not be there. He and his wife had left for the Dakotas about the same time Donald had gone West and no one had seen them since. The rest, daughter Christie, then Norman, Katie, Murdo Junior, and John, were within visiting distance of their parents on Ness Hill. What would they all be like now, seven years later? And what of Augusta McIver of Spring Hill? She had been a pretty thing of sixteen. She'd be a woman now.

The all too familiar sound of a train whistle brought him unhurriedly back to the station. It had been a long journey and he would be only too happy to leave train riding behind. For a while, at least.

For Sophia Morrison this Tuesday had been a day full of promises. She had promised herself to keep control and not get too flustered. Her husband, Murdo, had promised he would make it to the station in time and she would just have to abide by it. J. J. Jones, the station master, had promised her that the train from Sherbrooke would stop at his Echo Vale station even if he had to stand astride the tracks. She would have to abide by this promise too. Life, it seemed to her, had so many variables. Unable to do more, she sat down on a rough bench on the station veranda and waited, sure that Donald would be aboard the train today.

She had a good hour-and-a-half wait before the train's scheduled arrival. It was barely six o'clock in the evening and it wasn't due till at least seven-thirty. Patience, under such circumstances, was impossible, nor did she care for that matter.

Echo Vale, a main junction many years ago, was now merely a flag stop. The house, which was both station and post office, was located a mile or two up from Megantic where the Tenth Range Road crossed the tracks and meandered down to Sandy Bay. It wasn't much, but Sandy Bay had been a lively place when the Murdo Morrisons, Stewarts, McRitchies and John Cuisloch MacDonald had decided to strike out from Red Mountain and Lingwick and start pioneering all over again on better land. Megantic was a small slip of a settlement called Chaudière in the spring of 1855 when Murdo picked a goodly piece of property on Ness Hill with a view looking south across the lake, then cleared enough of it to sow a bushel of barley and potatoes. A modest log cabin went up and farm buildings followed. Donald had been born in 1858, right here atop Ness Hill, with the country-side spread out before him like a soft, down blanket.

The ear-piercing scream of a train whistle and the metallic screeching of heavy, slowing wheels grinding their way around the last bend in the tracks brought Sophia off the bench. Pulling her shawl around her shoulders, she moved over to the veranda steps, trembling with anticipation. As she reached them, J. J. Jones appeared from nowhere, his face bound up in one large grin. She looked up at him with soft, watery eyes and she couldn't speak. When she looked back the train was swinging down the tracks and her heart jumped: it seemed to be moving far too fast to stop. Then she felt a hand touch her elbow and she wondered if her feet would move.

TWO

SHOWDOWN

3

A PARCEL OF LAND

JULY 1886

Murdo Morrison leaned wearily against the split-rail fence, staring abjectly across the barren fields. The harsh words of his youngest son still rang in his ears. All at once he felt older than his seventy-four years and was conscious of the added weight of his body under the stooped shoulders. Looking down he saw his rough hands gripping the fence, hands gnarled like oak bark. His face, too, hidden beneath the dark felt cap, was laced with deep wrinkles; "furrows," as Sophia affectionately referred to them. He was getting old, and just when all seemed to be working out for the better, things went awry and Murdo Morrison could not quite understand why.

Three years before, Donald had come home from the West. Murdo had arrived at the Echo Vale station as his son stepped down from the coach. He stood back and watched their youngest stroll forward, wrapping his arms about his mother and lifting her off the ground. Even old Jones, the stationmaster, bounced around with renewed vigor, trying to wrest the suitcase from Donald's grip so he could support his mother with both hands. Yes, from that moment everything would be all right.

And it had been good. The first question Donald asked the next morning was about the trouble, in his quiet manner, his voice steady. Murdo looked at Sophia, who was busy with the dishes. His eyes swung back to his son, and he began.

"Debts" summed it up in one word. Donald nodded but said nothing as his father told him how down through the years he had always managed to help the sons and daughters, as they got married, to establish themselves in their own farms as well as keeping this place together on Ness Hill. It hadn't been easy, to be sure. There had always been family wrangling over the hundred acres of land; he'd quarreled with Murdo Junior years before when Donald was too young to know much about it. And there'd been lean, lean years on this farm, whose land grew better stones and rocks than vegetables and grain.

Donald listened attentively, then finally swung his cowboy boots up on a corner of the table. How much was the family debt now, he wanted to know. Murdo looked down at his hands. From the side of the room the dishes stopped rattling. The small log house went curiously quiet. Seven hundred dollars, Murdo said, the words hardly audible. A good portion of this he owed to a man from Montreal, George Burland, by name.

Donald paid the debts. Old Murdo felt good, and for almost two years the farm atop Ness Hill hummed with vitality. The forest was pushed back, fields rid of stones, new fangled implements appeared, and Sophia looked ten years younger. Mind, there were still upsets about the place, as in any other family. Murdo, not used to anything new, often criticized Donald's overspending, though the money was his son's. He also told Donald he didn't like the rumors drifting up from Megantic about his living it up at the American House. Such criticism didn't sit well with Donald.

One evening after chores Murdo asked Donald if he had ever thought of settling down, maybe with the young McIver girl from up Spring Hill way. For some reason, this had started Donald off—and he didn't even make it back for milking the next morning.

Then over the past year things had drifted downhill. He and Donald couldn't talk without arguing, and stubborn though he was, Murdo felt the farm slipping from his grasp, the very farm he had hacked out of the bush. Things came to a head when

Donald refused to draw any further on his depleted savings to help finance the farm. His father was not willing to give up control of the operation as he had long ago promised, Donald claimed. Murdo was too proud to beg his son for help and turned instead to another of his offspring, Murdo Junior, from whom he borrowed $300. Soon this sum was gone too and the other debts continued to pile up. And the farm was not making any money: there seemed no hope of paying his creditors.

In desperation Murdo had gone to a Megantic moneylender, Major Malcolm McAulay. On April 6, 1886, he had taken out a mortgage on the farm for $1,100. Of this transaction he had told Donald nothing. By now they were hardly speaking.

Donald had found out about it at the American House, which led to the ugly scene this July morning. Angry words were spilled. Murdo had walked away from it and stood by the fence looking down toward Lake Megantic. Behind him he heard a door slam. Donald was leaving again.

Augusta McIver stood out by the woodshed, hypnotized by the radiant colors cast by the setting sun. A small breeze fluttered the ends of her dark hair as she closed her eyes, trying to imagine the sunset before her. When she opened them, she was startled to find something blocking out the sun and her smile became part of the beauty of the moment. Donald Morrison reached out and touched her shoulders, his eyes fixed solidly on hers.

He had never failed to set a spark alive within her. Even as a teenager, when she saw him at church meetings and assemblies, he had held an intangible fascination which she could never put into words. When he was away for those long years it had never occurred to her there was anyone else in her life but Donald. They had frequently exchanged letters while apart and it delighted her recently when Donald, in a rare moment of emotion, told her he had kept all the letters she wrote to him while he was away.

Now he stood here before her, his mouth hardly visible beneath a thick brown mustache which swept by the corners of his lips to stop abruptly where the chin and neck joined. The mustache was one of the few vestiges of his years spent in the West; it, a pair of well-worn cowboy boots, and two Colt revolvers she knew he owned but seldom, if ever, referred to.

They walked down to the end of the garden and sat on the grass while she talked on about life there in Spring Hill, how only that day she had bumped into Finlay McLeod, the local hotel owner, who was asking about Donald's health. They laughed over her retelling of rumors she'd heard about him creating quite a stir around Megantic, most of it rousting about the taverns. These stories got better with every telling, he said with a laugh, as his fingers traced the outline of her shoulder through the thin cotton dress. Silence came between them, and at last he asked if she too had heard the problems he was having with his father. She nodded, feeling him wanting to talk.

Augusta had never heard the full story of what had taken place since Donald's return almost three years before. When minor aggravations arose between father and son, Donald often mentioned them briefly, then promptly seemed to forget them. Lately the mutual annoyance had become more prevalent, and these days instead of talking about them, Donald was harboring them deep inside. It was this sort of atmosphere which seemed to come between him and Augusta, prolonging the time until they might settle down together. After all, she wasn't "getting any younger," as members of her own family reminded her from time to time. Donald had been promised the Morrison farm, that being part of his agreement to stay in the East, but it hadn't seemed to work out that way. Even now he was telling her how twice he had made offers to his parents; first, that for $400 he would give up his claim to the farm, then raising it to $900 because of additional time and money he had put into the property. Murdo Morrison flatly turned these down. Instead he offered Donald $100, plus expenses back to the West. Donald countered by suggesting he take the farm and give Murdo a first mortgage of $500. Added to this he would give his parents a house on several acres of land and supply them with firewood, a cow, and six or seven sheep.

Murdo had thought it over and actually *accepted* it. But Sophia hadn't. She told both her husband and son that she had settled down for the last time and wouldn't be rooted up again.

Even Augusta knew that the place on Ness Hill was too large
for the old couple; the offer of a smaller place on their own, with
only one cow to milk and a kitchen garden to tend to, would be
perfect. But then, Augusta McIver knew more about Donald's
father than Donald gave her credit for, much of it concerning
the old man's constant disputes over the same farm with his
other sons when Donald was out West. They had spread all over
the country. At one time Malcolm, the eldest son, had received a
quitclaim deed from his father, giving the son the farm in exchange for looking after it. Murdo later got the deed back, then
turned to Murdo Junior to help him out. With more flare-ups
and family distrust (Murdo Junior threw it all over and bought
the farm across the road), the parents then pleaded for their
youngest son to come home and "settle matters."

There was talk, too, that Malcolm had sued his father and
finally *fled* West, where he and his wife settled in Crystal, in
the northern Dakotas, far from the dour, stubborn Scot who
clung to his land tighter than he ever would to his own family.

In a moment of impulse Augusta touched the sleeve of
Donald's cotton shirt, feeling a warmth flooding through her. He
stopped talking, looked at her, and smiled. After a moment he
told her what had led up to the sudden outburst with Murdo
that morning. At first he thought the story of the mortgage was a
joke, his friends were having him on. But when his father admitted the truth, he was faced with the sudden realization that all
the money, time, and effort he'd put into that very farm might
come to naught. He had stormed down to Megantic for legal advice and to get a writ to protect his interest in the place. It was
sheer idiocy to deal with a moneylender like McAulay, Donald
said to Augusta, as he worked himself into a rage. Then his voice
trailed off.

In the ensuing silence Augusta wondered to herself how, in
such a closely knit family, water could so often run thicker than
Scottish blood. Now, listening to Donald, she knew full well that
the enmity which had earlier risen between Murdo Morrison and
his other sons was about to be repeated with his youngest. This
very thought made her shiver anew and she drew herself closer
to him.

Malcolm B. McAulay stretched across his massive mahogany desk, flipped the numeral card of the desk calendar to read Tuesday, the sixth of July, then settled deep into the large leather chair. As his head reclined against the soft back he fastened his eyes on his friend George Burland who sat across the room. Only then did McAulay pick up their conversation where the wrongly dated calendar had interrupted him. If, he said in a low, even tone, young Morrison was in such a huff, he got into it all by himself. He should have stayed in the Northwest where he obviously belonged and saved all the anguish he caused hereabouts.

George Burland sat stiff in the chair, nodding wisely as McAulay shifted himself again by propping a knee against the edge of the desk. To Burland, Malcolm was a bundle of latent energy, seemingly always on the verge of exploding at the slightest thing, yet having that certain facility of controlling those emotions.

Though only thirty-nine years old, McAulay looked more like a man in his mid-forties, due in part to the harsh, clean lines of his tailored dark suit and austere white shirt. His manner was abrupt and confident and left very little room for the option of argument. Most people, thought Burland, watching his friend closely, would find him attractive, though closer inspection would reveal a nose which was slightly too small for his face and a mustache too large. Women did consider him charming; his friends and business associates knew him to be blunt and quite often uncompromising.

Burland had listened to McAulay recite his past many times. He had been born in Ross-shire, Scotland, in 1847, and come to Canada with his parents at age four. At eighteen his sense of adventure took him to the embattled United States where he joined the Union Army in the last year of the Civil War and fought field to field, bayonet to bayonet, under Major General George Henry Thomas. After the conflict he returned home to the Eastern Townships to channel his energies into lumber, real estate, and activities with the local Megantic militia. George Burland, himself from Montreal, had met McAulay through business contacts. He found the latter to be generous with those he liked, but utterly ruthless with those who got in his way. McAulay, for some reason, had taken a liking to Burland, pushing deals, mainly mortgages, his way. Burland found that Malcolm McAulay ran everything in a regimented way as though he were still in the Union Army. His title of "major" came not from active service but rather from his militia connections.

What set McAulay's nerves on edge this morning, however, was Burland's news of Donald Morrison's writ of execution against the family farm, in an obvious attempt to wrest it away from his father. From what he could gather, Morrison sought $900 as payment for work done on the farm for the past two and a half years and for monies of his own used to pay off farm debts. To this McAulay grunted and opening a desk drawer drew out a sheet of paper which he fired off in Burland's general direction. Burland picked it up, noticing it to be a mortgage, duly signed by Murdo on April 6, 1886. Burland read further:

". . . Murdoch Morrison Senior, farmer, at said village of Megantic, who in our presence acknowledged to owe and to be justly and truly indebted unto Major Malcolm B. McAulay, Esquire, Trader, of the said village of Megantic, in the sum of eleven hundred dollars currency . . . which said sum of money the said Debtor hereby promises to pay or cause to be paid to said Creditor, his heirs or assigns, in one year from this date, with interest at the rate of nine per centum per annum. . . ."

Burland returned the paper to the desk without reading on. For a moment he looked at the smiling McAulay, wondering to himself what would happen if the court upheld Donald Morrison's claim to the farm in lieu of the $900 payment from his father. The case would definitely be worth following.

4

SCALES OF JUSTICE

SEPTEMBER 1886–FEBRUARY 1887

The summer of 1886 had been anything but pleasant for Donald Morrison. The business of suing his father was a sickening one. But his lawyer, a man named McLean with the Sherbrooke firm of Hall, White & Cate, had assured him there was no alternative solution.

Morrison had also been to Montreal seeking legal advice, but no one in the profession could agree what action should be taken, other than to sue. McLean, a small, round-faced man, made application with the court in Sherbrooke, and a date for the hearing was set for mid-July. As it turned out, Murdo Morrison failed to appear in court on that date, and following a discussion between the judge and Donald's legal counsel, the court established that the father was obliged to pay the $900, plus court costs which came to $47.50. Ashamed at having taken advantage of his aging father, Donald paid the costs himself, though he knew he could not have settled for anything less than $900. His father would grudgingly have to pay for it out of the mortgage money borrowed from McAulay.

Arriving home in Megantic late, he told his father what had taken place and what was due him. His father, his eyes bleak and weary, replied he couldn't pay his son. When Donald suggested he take it from the McAulay loan, Murdo said he

never did get all of it. Besides, he had already repaid Murdo
Junior $300 he had borrowed some time ago. But surely he still
had $800 . . . ?

Murdo shook his head. McAulay had kept back half that
amount, he answered, his short arms dangling pathetically at his
side. The rest had gone to pay his other debts. Donald shrugged
and turned to his mother, asking for the mortgage contract.
Finding it in the bottom of the trunk, she gave it to him, her face
pinched and discolored, unable to cope with the confusion.

Donald read it through, his attention drawn to a scribbled
note at the bottom in McAulay's handwriting. It stated that the
remaining $400 would be paid to Murdo three months after the
date of the mortgage or kept as partial repayment of the $1,100.
Puzzled, Donald read it again and again, coming to the only conclusion he could think of: McAulay was merely withholding the
$400 to avoid paying the entire sum, while at the same time ex-
acting a 9 per cent interest on the entire $1,100. Unable to read
English, or Gaelic either, for that matter, his father took it for
granted that nothing was amiss.

The remainder of the summer passed like a worsening nightmare. Donald confronted McAulay on many occasions as he
tried to show the moneylender that he was swindling his father.
All the time his lawyer, McLean, told him not to worry, things
would settle in his favor. Mystified by the evasiveness of legal
parlance, Donald kept insisting that the situation was getting
worse. Too, how could an old man who was earning nothing,
keep up payments on such an enormous sum?

As the time dragged on, Donald watched his savings, and patience, eaten away. After much deliberation with his colleagues,
McLean said it was time Donald took the initiative. After all, he
told his client, it was already September and now was the moment to do the unexpected—he suggested they force the farm to
a sheriff's sale because the present stalemate between McAulay's
so-called mortgage and Donald's court judgment against his father was only costing in legal fees and wasted time. Donald
didn't understand. McLean explained. By forcing the farm to
sheriff's auction, Donald would be able to purchase the property
and, with this settled, could then take on McAulay's contro-
versial mortgage. The mortgage was invalid because his father

owed *him* $900 for the years of work on the farm and equipment purchased *before* money was borrowed from McAulay. In other words, Donald's claim took priority. But, Donald wanted to know, what if McAulay outbid them at the auction? McLean shook his head. All the moneylender wanted was to protect his investment by continuing to collect on the mortgage as it fell due. Donald finally agreed to McLean's suggestion, against his better judgment. But then lawyers were supposed to know things like that.

The auction was set for September 18 in Cookshire, in the county of Compton, some forty miles from Megantic. Donald, arriving early with his lawyer, was dressed conservatively in a dark suit which crowded him about the shoulders, dusty black boots, and a white shirt with a stiff rounded collar and a somber four-in-hand tie. He was clearly uncomfortable as he listened to the final instructions from McLean: the lawyer would do all the bidding. Donald nodded and was glancing abstractedly at the door, when McAulay entered along with George Burland and several other men. At 11 A.M. sharp Sheriff Bowen took his place and the auction began.

As McLean had predicted earlier, McAulay began by opposing this sale by default; all he wanted was to protect his investment. His expenses alone amounted to $217, he grumbled . . . ! Bowen nodded and turned to Donald. McLean stood up, immediately starting the bidding at $200.

Donald's head swung toward McAulay, watching the man's thoughtful expression. He saw the lips move and heard the counterbid: $1,000. Donald's mouth dropped open. A sense of sheer hopelessness replaced any shred of confidence he might have had in his lawyer. But McLean's confident manner remained intact. He looked steadfastly at the sheriff, nodding, raising the bid to $1,100. Sheriff Bowen then shifted his attention to McAulay.

Donald Morrison felt his fingernails scratching deep into his clenched fists. Two thoughts entered his mind simultaneously: would McAulay bid higher and how could he, Donald, raise $1,100 even if McAulay held off? His heart began pounding. He watched McAulay's expressionless face, then caught the head moving from side to side: the bidding was over.

McLean tittered beside him. Sheriff Bowen came 'round to

them. The farm was Morrison's . . . for $1,100. Now would that be cash or check? McLean stepped forward, whispering to the sheriff that his client would need three days to raise the money. Bowen shook his head, reminding McLean this was an *auction* sale. Cash on the barrel. Cash? The word whirled around in Morrison's brain as he watched McAulay step forward with his check book. The sheriff shrugged, told McLean he was sorry, but he would have to accept McAulay's original bid. The crafty major had certainly outwitted lawyer McLean. Not only had he protected his investment but he had gained a farm in the bargain.

Donald sought later to appeal the sheriff's decision. McLean agreed, but demanded that his fees be paid first. The appeal was postponed several times as Donald vainly looked for another counsel. Finally, on Thursday, February 3, 1887, the Sherbrooke firm of Yves, Brown & French filed for an order of possession for their client, Malcolm McAulay. The sale was upheld. The Morrisons' holdings on lots 75 and 76 in the township of Whitton were gone—lock, stock, and barrel.

5

DUQUETTE'S NEW PLACE

JULY 1887

On the hot, sunny afternoon of Tuesday the fifth of July, 1887, Auguste Duquette, a small, compact French-Canadian farmer, stood poised with indecision on the veranda of the American House in Megantic, his eyes fixed on the open front door. His appointment, elsewhere, was drawing close, but the thought of a cool beer in the tavern made him hesitate.

For a moment he turned toward the street, watching a curl of dust spiral upward, then move away at right angles to the building. *Damn* hot, he thought to himself as he ran a thickening tongue across his parched lips. The day was a scorcher. Even after the short walk from the driving shed to the veranda, his brow was bathed in sweat. He knew the futility of wiping it with the sleeve of his shirt—it would be just as wet a minute later. His only course of action, then, was to put up with the heat—and slip inside for a quick one. If he hurried, he could make the appointment on time and still have a beer. He swung around, stepped across the weathered veranda, and stopped, his conscience the only barrier between him and the hotel. He had told his wife and three children he wanted to come alone to Megantic, complete the deal, and then return directly. But it was a big moment, they told him, and they wanted to share it with him.

But Auguste used the heat of the day as an excuse and he came alone, enjoying a rare moment of tranquillity.

Within an hour of leaving home, Duquette's horse and buggy had clattered over the well-worn planks of the bridge which spanned the Chaudière between Agnes and Megantic. As the thin metal rims of the wheels jolted down onto the hard-packed dirt of Maple Street, the French Canadian looked up to see Megantic spread out in a rising cluster of buildings shimmering in the searing afternoon sun. On reaching the town square, he turned his horse to the right and headed for the railway station where he would discharge the first of his commissions, paying off several freight bills. Two hours later he had tethered his horse in the shed behind the American House, with only one remaining chore to take care of. Well, maybe two.

Though a handful of hotels flourished in Megantic, Leet's on Maple, the main thoroughfare, and Pope's, directly opposite, were the most favored among the local townsfolk. Duquette preferred Pope's, or the American House, to use its formal name. It was owned and operated by Albert W. Pope, a benevolent town father whom Auguste Duquette considered a friend. Besides, the hotel's structure had always impressed the French Canadian, with its high but modest false front, two storys, and pillared balcony which overhung this same veranda where he now stood.

He licked his lips once more and went in the door.

Inside, Duquette found the large room filled with Scots, a people he found mildly fascinating. Though some spoke English, and fewer spoke French, the majority conversed in a language called Gaelic which made no tolerable sense to the French Canadian. During frequent trips to town, Duquette would invariably stop at Pope's on the way home, just to watch these Scots band together at the bar, where they would sing and laugh uproariously, slapping each other on the backs and carrying on with such merriment they must have been heard clear to the Maine border. Get them outside, however, and they were a quiet folk who went unhurriedly about their tasks.

Among the crush of tables and Scots, Auguste Duquette spied a friend sitting alone at a corner table. Télesphore Legendre, a former millowner, greeted him happily, pulling out a chair for him as Auguste went looking for a couple of beers.

Duquette enjoyed the chatter which followed and was on his third draught when he felt a hand settle heavily on his shoulder. He looked up to see a man he recognized as Donald Graham. Graham was about to yank him out of the chair, yelling over the din that McAulay was waiting for him, *if* Duquette had nothing better to do . . . ! Duquette felt himself moving upward when Télesphore Legendre reached over to his nearest shoulder and eased him back down in his chair again. Auguste hadn't finished his beer, shouted Legendre with a grin, so hadn't Graham better get back and tell his friend McAulay that he'd be over shortly? Graham shrugged, then quickly disappeared in the crowd.

Legendre's smile left his face as Graham departed. Duquette looked bleakly at Legendre, who moved in close and began telling him how the entire town knew why he was in town. Legendre, who prided himself on never butting into other's affairs, felt Duquette should be warned about the property he was about to buy. Leave it well enough alone, he pleaded with Duquette, let the Scots feud over it, and don't get involved. Didn't Auguste understand?

The former miller leaned back, watching the happiness drain from Duquette's face. He knew how Auguste had scrimped and saved for a real place of his own and thought the one McAulay had shown him was perfect. Even Duquette's wife thought it a palace. But surely he could see it wasn't a good choice. There were *other* farms . . .

Duquette shook his head. He had offered McAulay $1,500 for the old Morrison place. McAulay asked for a little more and Duquette had accepted the offer. Yes, today he would sign the papers. . . .

Legendre nodded. But surely Duquette wouldn't do such a thing if he knew the whole story. The bit about the telegraph poles and all? Duquette put down his glass. What about them?

Legendre sighed, waited for a moment, then leaned forward. It seems, he said, that four such poles had been left lying on the Morrison place last fall while young Morrison was still legally on the place trying to get an appeal against the auction sale. Yes, Duquette knew of the sale. Well, with Morrison's parents moved temporarily to a disused school house, he held onto the farm and happened to come across the poles. Not knowing whose they were or why they were there, he cut them up, using them for firewood. But they turned out to be McAulay's and McAulay had Morrison arrested. Morrison'd have gone to jail too, if he hadn't paid the $50 fine for cutting up the poles. And when he got back to the farm, young Morrison found the family furniture gone; he traced it to two men and a boy who said they'd done only what McAulay ordered. So Morrison in turn had McAulay arrested for "forcible entry."

Legendre continued, mentioning how McAulay's trial on the charge of forcible entry was delayed three times when the witnesses, the two men and the boy, failed to appear. The case was finally dropped, leaving Morrison seething with frustration.

As Auguste Duquette listened, he felt his whole world collapsing around him. Sure he'd heard rumors too that Morrison vowed no one would live on that farm, but it wasn't *his* fight. It was for sale, legally, and he wanted to buy it and he wanted to yell all this at Legendre, but he knew his friend just wanted to put him straight on the matter.

Duquette, flushed from the beer, stood up to leave, then leaned across the table toward Télesphore Legendre. Where were all the Morrisons now, he wanted to know. Legendre smiled, hoping Duquette might consider the advice he'd given him. Well, as far as he'd heard, Murdo and Sophia had lived in the abandoned schoolhouse till this spring when their daughter Christie and her husband, Alex MacArthur, over near Marsden, gave them some land nearby where friends and relatives built them a small log house. Donald had helped with the move and building, then went back to the Ness Hill farm. Legendre paused, waiting for some reaction from Duquette. When he got none, he added that last month, June, Donald Morrison had finally been moved out with the sheriff's help and . . .

Before Legendre could finish, Duquette had turned and left without so much as a nod.

Though Legendre didn't see Auguste Duquette for some time following their conversation at Pope's, he learned that Duquette had indeed bought the old Morrison farm. Details of the transaction were sketchy, but it seemed he paid $1,608 for it, with $1,230 down and the remaining $378 to be paid over the next four years, with interest at 8 per cent. Duquette had moved with his family onto the farm within three days of signing the papers. In the meantime, there was talk that Donald Morrison had repeated his threat to prevent anyone from setting foot on the place. But then, what could the young Scot do about it now?

6

FIT TO KILL

APRIL–JUNE 1888

On the morning of Tuesday the third of April, 1888, Auguste
Duquette slipped silently out of bed, dressed, and was about his
chores well before dawn. For the first time this year he could
smell spring in the air, despite the lingering drifts of snow. However, mentally planning for his crops had kept him awake half
the night and he was out early, eagerly pacing about his land.

By eleven o'clock in the morning, and still without breakfast,
Duquette paused to lean against the split-rail fence bordering
the Tenth Range Road. To his surprise he saw a tall man, a
stranger to him, coming up the road. He smiled in neighborly
fashion but his expression soon changed when the man introduced himself as Donald Morrison and stayed only long enough
to tell the French-Canadian farmer that he expected him off the
property within the next ten days.

This unexpected encounter left Auguste Duquette more be-
wildered than frightened. For the past eight or nine months the
Duquette family had lived peacefully on their new farm with no
sign of trouble. During one of Duquette's many winter trips into
Megantic for supplies he had casually asked about Morrison and
was told that the ex-cowboy had high-tailed it for Montreal in
late fall and hadn't been seen since. Duquette had prayed he

would remain there, but obviously his prayer had not been answered.

Among Donald Morrison's closest friends in Megantic was a boyhood chum, Murdo Beaton, an oft-times humorous man of Scottish stock whose strength was well hidden behind a modest nature. Murdo was of medium height, about five feet nine inches, with a thick, broad chest and a pair of powerful legs. His arms, on close inspection, were somewhat too short to balance his heavy torso, but they served him well for his work as a quarryman. Indeed, it was the fun-loving pair of Morrison and Norman MacAulay who a decade earlier tried talking Murdo into going West. He had declined; he could make more money, he said, by working the quarries of Maine and Vermont where many Canadians were already piling up their fortunes. When Morrison returned East in 1883 he was surprised to find his friend Beaton still boasting how he'd make it down there. But Beaton's trips to the States were short; his love for his Canadian home overshadowed his desire to make it rich below the border.

Now, in 1888, Morrison had returned to the Eastern Townships on the first day of April following a winter of discontent. Though he hadn't given up hope of getting the Megantic farm back, he'd met one frustration after another. Lawyers from Sherbrooke and Montreal sympathized with him, admitting openly it was quite unfair that he should lose both payment for his years of work and the actual cash he'd personally put into the farm. But, they said, off the cuff, he had been given bad legal advice, and now, with the sale transaction long since complete and Morrison's final appeal quashed, he had little hope of recouping so much as a blade of grass. It was now obvious to him that the law refused to deal fairly with losses. He felt there was but one course left to follow. So he had confronted Duquette in his own field and told him to get out.

On the morning of the sixteenth of April, a Monday, Morrison ran into Murdo Beaton outside Malcom Matheson's general store on Maple Street. They clapped each other on the back, swapped a few stories, and were about to go their separate ways when Morrison suggested a short walk. Beaton eyed him quizzically; his idea of a short stroll differed greatly from Morrison's, he knew from experience. A walk of short duration might begin at sunrise and end at sunset for Morrison. To Beaton such a trek was a week's journey, or at least would seem like it. But no, Morrison said it would only involve an hour or two, and besides, the return trip was all down hill.

Duquette was finishing some needed repairs in the barn when the pair entered. He couldn't recognize them at first, as they stood there with their backs to the sunlit door, so he moved away at an angle and leaned against his pitchfork. Only then did he realize it was Morrison, along with Beaton, from Megantic.

Morrison's second confrontation with Duquette was as brief as the first and his message also: get off the farm. Beaton, standing off to the side, waited for a response. Duquette obliged him with a shrug of the shoulders and told Morrison that he'd paid for the farm and he wouldn't leave. All three stood motionless for a moment, till Morrison looked at Beaton and nodded; then they left. The pair headed back for Megantic, talking about old times.

By May the days were noticeably longer. Winter was finally admitting defeat and had retreated, leaving small pockets of snow to fend for themselves. Soon robins appeared, along with purple finches, blue jays, martins, and nuthatches, while high above, the Canada geese seemed to stride across the sky with the steady pace of long-distance runners.

By the eighth, a Tuesday, Auguste Duquette was in fine spirits. Spring planting had begun early, his fences were mended, and his stock—a horse, four cows, two pigs, ten hens, and a calf—had survived the winter without complaints. Both of Morrison's visits to the farm had worried him though, until finally, the week before, he had dropped in to see Major McAulay, telling him what had taken place. The major exploded with anger, shouting loud enough to be heard out on the street. This sort of behavior would surely land Morrison in jail, and should it occur again, McAulay said, waving a finger under Duquette's nose, they would get satisfaction through the chief constable and put an end to it.

But by Tuesday the incident with Morrison seemed like a bad dream, leaving Duquette free to till and sow without worry.

And that night he had worked well past dinnertime almost without noticing it. He quit at nine, however, when tired muscles in his arms, legs, and shoulders reminded him it was enough for the day. By nine-thirty the Duquette household had settled down, and Auguste, habitually a light sleeper, was snoring almost before his head reached the pillow.

Past midnight he awoke with a start to find the room swirling in a flickering red glow. Mon dieu, he thought, sitting bolt upright, the house is on fire!

Leaping out of bed, he was at the window in two bounds. Flames were engulfing the stable. Duquette bolted back, screaming for his three children and wife to get out; the house might be next. But luckily a light breeze sweeping in from the southeast fanned the flames and sparks away from the log building, sending them harmlessly out across the fields. It was far too late, however, to save the stable—or the animals trapped inside.

News of Duquette's loss swept the countryside, and many an accusing finger pointed at Donald Morrison. It was widely known he had publicly announced that he would get the French Canadian off his land. And when word was circulated that Morrison had twice gone to the farm to tell Duquette to leave, it was all but a foregone conclusion that the ex-cowboy was responsible. There was, however, more excitement to come.

On Thursday night of the following week, May 17, Auguste Duquette, his wife, and the three children were sitting about the kitchen when a deafening roar of a rifle and crash of splintering glass sent them scurrying to the floor. Trembling with fear, Mme. Duquette and the children watched as her husband reached up gingerly to blow out the lamp then scramble across the glass-strewn floor to the front window. Peering over the sill he saw the shadow of a man standing by the barn with a rifle. Slowly the rifle moved upward, then steadied, and a second explosion rocked the small room as the slug tore through the door, missing Duquette by four or five feet, and buried itself in the far wall. Later, when peace returned to the small log house, Duquette managed to dig out the first slug, which had smashed the old clock and lodged itself in its face. The hands had stopped at nine-thirty.

Early the next morning Duquette went directly to the police office in the Megantic town hall. He recounted exactly what had taken place, down to the last detail. He complained that he and his family hadn't slept well since the stable fire and . . . for Duquette, promises of protection weren't enough. He feared for the life of his family—and for himself. He even said he knew who had done the shooting; he could tell from the way the man walked.

Returning home, Duquette found his family almost beside themselves with fear. The burning of the stable and now the possibility of being murdered in their beds was too much for them. Mme. Duquette demanded that they find another place to stay until this wave of violence was over. Her husband was shaken. He would not give up a place he had worked so hard to obtain. Then, seeing his wife was close to tears, he stepped forward, putting his arms gently around her shoulders.

By late afternoon Mme. Duquette and the children were safely installed across the road at the neighbors'. Ironically, those neighbors were Murdo Junior and Marion Morrison, Donald's brother and sister-in-law. Being caught in the middle of the situation for them was just one more heartbreaking episode in the tragic history of that farm. Their new friend, Auguste Duquette, had declined to stay himself. Refusing to desert his home, he had left to defend it as soon as his family had got settled. His wife had made him promise, however, that he would arrange to have someone remain with him.

No one was overly enthusiastic about his request, though finally he was able to persuade a friend to stay with him the first night. Finding others for subsequent nights was almost impossible, and finally within a week and a few days he had run out of volunteers, which forced him to stay the evenings of May 28 and 29 in town. Returning to the farm early the morning of Wednesday, the thirtieth, he had barely reached the driveway when he smelled smoke. He convinced himself at first it was smoldering wood left over from the burned stable, but then, as he ran around a section of woods and out into the field, he was greeted with the sight of a jumbled pile of black, smoking timbers where his house had been.

Augusta McIver stepped off the porch into the darkness, pulling the wool shawl tightly about her shoulders. After glancing back to make sure she hadn't been seen, she gathered up her long dress with both hands and ran down to the road. Actually she couldn't care less who saw her, for at this moment she only had Donald on her mind.

The burning of the Duquette house on Ness Hill several days before had been a blow to her, but nothing like the thunderbolt that struck when she heard that the local coroner was completing an investigation which would surely culminate in Donald's arrest. How could the law be so biased against a man who had suffered so much ill treatment? Donald had lost his money and his farm, and now he was fast becoming the scapegoat for a series of incidents which had *nothing* to do with him.

This morning, Monday, June 4, she had gone shopping in Megantic with her parents and younger sister and found the entire town in an uproar. Word was going the rounds that A. G. Woodward, coroner for the district of St. Francis, had called an "inquest" (or inquiry) into the fires and rifle shots at Duquette's. This would have been fair enough, but it seemed everyone who had been asked to submit depositions had something to say about Donald Morrison. At least, that's what Murdo Beaton told her.

Augusta had taken leave of her family to shop on her own, when she saw Murdo step from Antoine Roy's blacksmith shop down the street. He waved at her and came up briskly. She liked Murdo Beaton and immediately slipped her arm through his, causing not a few raised eyebrows as they walked along.

Her smile of greeting had faded with his first few words: Donald was being openly accused of arson and attempted murder. Stunned, she clung to Beaton, her eyes cast to the ground. He told her of the inquest set two days hence, about the testimony which had already been taken, with at least one man claiming he'd lent a rifle to Donald not two days before the shots were fired into Duquette's kitchen. It was rumored that another, maybe one of Donald's sisters, would testify in a written disposition that they had heard Donald swear he would get Duquette off the land. And there were other things . . . Murdo's voice trailed off with emotion. He felt Augusta's hand clench tightly on his arm.

Before they parted Augusta made Murdo promise he would find Donald, who was cautiously awaiting the outcome of the inquest, and have him meet her tonight. Murdo cocked his head to

one side, paused, and nodded. He would try, he said, and where
would she be? She managed to smile. Donald would know, she
said.

When she found him, Donald Morrison was bent over the
small stream splashing his face with water. His crouched figure
was caught between the night shadow of a large oak and a patch
of bright moonlight. Augusta stood motionless for a moment as
the water sprayed up around him. She'd caught him off guard,
she mused to herself, the great frontiersman caught . . . !

"*De man a tha sibh?*" ("How are you?") he said with a laugh,
not bothering to turn around. Augusta caught her breath and
leaned against the tree, quite taken by surprise. "*Theid thu
ifrinn*," she answered in Gaelic, telling him to go to the devil. He
stood up with his face still dripping and lunged to grab the
shawl and dry his face. But she was too quick and, with a laugh,
asked how he could have heard her, what with all the splashing
and his back to her. He said it wasn't too difficult to pick up the
sound of a team of plow horses, and they both laughed as they
stepped deeper into Ayre's sugarbush.

Augusta told him about the coroner's inquiry. She was deeply
worried about the hearing's possible outcome. If foul play was
found to be responsible for the unfortunate events out at the old
Morrison farm, it was probable Donald would be indicted—
everyone knew of his threats to the French-Canadian family.
Augusta probed this delicate subject with care, not wishing to
give Donald the impression she doubted him. She asked him
about the burning of the stable, and her question brought a
chuckle from him. No, he said, he hadn't done it, for he had been
out courting a certain young lady from Spring Hill that very evening. She laughed, remembering it was so. She felt better then.
And the gunshots through the window? Donald shook his head,
promising he hadn't done it. And before she could speak again,
he told her he was in the Hampden area, south of Bury, the
night the Duquette house burned to the ground. And she and everyone else would have to take his word for it.

On the morning of Wednesday, the sixth of June 1888, the
village of Megantic was in a frenzy. Maple Street was alive with
horses and buggies and people who were scurrying about shop-

ping so they could get to the town hall before it was filled. Anyone arriving there after nine o'clock found they couldn't get a toe in the door, let alone find space on the stairs leading to the council chamber above where the inquest was to be held.

Woodward, the coroner, had scheduled the inquiry into the Duquette affair for 10 A.M. Everybody in town seemed to have turned up and the chamber became so crowded that even the witnesses had trouble finding a place to stand.

The coroner began with a brief summary of what had occurred, ending his account with the burning of the Duquette house, and as he spoke, in a deep, sonorous tone, his eyes swept the room, making sure all the witnesses were present. Murdo Beaton had been the last one and he now stood to the left of the stairway next to the McIver girl.

Roderick McRitchie, a farmer from the Whitton area, a slim, taciturn man, was first to take the stand. Under the quiet questioning of Woodward he said how Donald Morrison had vowed to him he'd take the law into his own hands. Woodward wanted to know when the conversation took place. Two weeks before the stable burned down, McRitchie said.

Norman McDonald, a carpenter from nearby Spalding township, came next. He testified that about a month before Morrison had come to his place and he added: "I loaned him a rifle, government rifle, and charged him to take good care of it." McDonald paused, looked at Woodward, adding, "I also loaned him ten cartridges."

During the testimony which followed, not a sound was heard. The spectators hung on every word spoken by the witnesses. They watched eagerly as several others testified to hearing Morrison say he'd get rid of "the Frenchman." John F. McDonald swore the same. Marion Morrison, Murdo Junior's wife, told a hushed council chamber that Donald declared something would happen if Duquette remained on the farm. This statement she swore to, and as she stepped down, the coroner called for a recess; the proceedings would recommence at one o'clock.

After lunch Woodward called Marion Morrison back to the stand. He asked her if she ever saw her brother-in-law carrying a gun. Yes, she answered, a revolver. And did she see him prior to the burning of the stable? Yes, he had come for supper and then left early. Woodward nodded, made some notes, then asked her if she had anything else to say. Marion nodded. "My husband said to me that Donald had threatened us with vengeance if we did not mind our own business. . . ." As Marion stepped down, a murmur went through the crowd, but it was difficult to know whether it was caused by what she had said or by the identity of the next witness, now approaching the stand.

Auguste Duquette felt strange in these surroundings. He stood nervously, waiting for the coroner to speak. When Woodward asked when he had first encountered Morrison, the French Canadian had difficulty speaking. He was told to take his time. By the time he told of Morrison's second threat, he had warmed to his role and clearly enjoyed being the center of interest. And what did Morrison say? the coroner asked. Duquette replied: "He said, 'You had no business to buy the place from McAulay. Now I shall say no more about it . . . you will move quicker than you got in.'"

Over by the stairway Murdo Beaton grumbled to himself, then turned to Augusta. Donald had said no such thing, he told her, his face flushed with anger. She nodded without taking her eyes off Duquette, who was remembering aloud the night the stable burned and again when the first bullet crashed through the window. She watched his eyes widen as he said, "And another struck the face of the clock right on the figure marked three. It came four or five feet near me." Duquette stopped for a moment, wiping an arm across his forehead. Then he continued, "I did not go out. I was afraid of being shot." From behind him someone coughed, breaking his line of thought. He stood for a moment looking blankly out over the crowd, trying to collect the words. The coroner waited patiently. Then Duquette started again, saying how on the night of the shooting he saw a man going behind the barn to a pile of stones and later saw the same man moving back to the barn. Did he recognize him? the coroner asked. Duquette nodded vigorously. "By his appearance and his walk and motions," he said, almost in a whisper, "I believe that person to be Donald Morrison." Shuffling feet and murmurs broke the silence. Duquette looked around to see the coroner lifting his hand for silence, then nodded at the French Canadian. "I . . . remember his hat," Duquette went on. "It was a peculiar

one and in fact . . . I have no . . . doubt . . . that person was
. . . Donald Morrison."

No further testimony held the impact of Auguste Duquette's
words. From then on, the crowd in the council chamber became
alive, giving Woodward the additional task of trying to keep
order. Finally, with the last witness stepping down from the
stand, he announced he would make public his decision within
the next few days.

He was true to his word. On Friday, June 8, Woodward issued a warrant for the arrest of Donald Morrison, charging him
with arson and shooting with intent to kill.

News of his impending arrest left Donald Morrison dazed.
He had been on his way to Megantic to hear the outcome of the
inquiry when he stopped by a modest homestead belonging to a
Scots settler who was a close friend of his father's. The old man
looked at him warily, then stuck out his hand. Donald clasped it,
feeling the bony fingers in his. He motioned for Donald to join
him in his cabin, where they sat down for a small taste of spirits.
Once settled, he asked Morrison where he might be going. When
the latter said on to Megantic, the old man shook his head. He
then told him about the warrant. Morrison shrugged and took a
sip from the mug. Arson? For what? He hadn't burned down
anything, nor had he shot at anyone, either, though he'd have
trouble confirming where he was the night the house burned
down. But there was little sense to it. They could *accuse* him of
what they liked, but they would have to prove it. The old man
shook his head vigorously, wishing this young lad good luck.

For the next three days Donald Morrison roamed the countryside, not knowing which way to turn. It had been foolish to
bother McAulay and threaten Duquette; *stupid* to do so openly.
He'd only wanted to scare them, but now these rash outbursts,
spoken in moments of utter frustration, were being blown horri-
bly out of proportion. Two years before, in 1886, he had been almost beside himself, watching his savings dwindle away, and
when the end came he couldn't convince himself that he hadn't
been duped by both McAulay and his *own* lawyers. He was also
convinced that by rights the land was still his and his father's;
he'd simply wait until the situation cleared itself up. In the
meantime he would let *no* constable put him away in jail.

Charged with arson and attempted murder? It was nothing but a joke.

Night brought a haze to the valley as Morrison climbed up to the road above Sandy Bay. Within fifteen minutes he had reached Echo Vale Cemetery at John Boston's corner, where the main road to Marsboro intersected the Drumavack Road to Spring Hill. John "Boston" MacDonald (so called because he'd once been to Boston and the nickname separated him from other John MacDonalds in the area) was still awake, the small wood house was ablaze with light. Walking softly by the cemetery, he then headed on the double toward Spring Hill. It was almost midnight when he finally awakened Augusta McIver.

They sat in the front room and talked long into the night, about the inquest and the warrant. Finally she tried persuading him to give himself up, but her words trailed off when she saw the skin around his jaws tighten. How could he, when the law hadn't satisfied any of his other claims? Why should it change now? And the ridiculous rumors that he vowed to shoot anyone who got in his way? She was the only one he'd talked to, apart from a small homesteader, so how could he have said such things? Suddenly they heard movement on the stairs, and stiffened, but it was only Augusta's father coming down to the kitchen. He passed by as though he hadn't seen them, and when they were alone once more Morrison told her how he'd still wanted the farm, buildings or no buildings. But he wouldn't get it by giving himself up. "Intent to kill"—that was just down the line from "murder." For a moment he was silent. Augusta leaned back against the couch, looking at his strong features outlined in the glow from the lamp in the hallway. At last he turned to her, his face etched with anger. Surely it was time someone stood up to the likes of McAulay. The man had had his way about the settlements too long. Augusta reached forward to touch his face with her fingers and she nodded, knowing full well that he was right.

If Donald couldn't say it better, an editorial soon after in the Montreal *Star* put the situation into perspective:

> To understand this state of affairs it
> must be stated that the people of the

> Scotch settlements declare they have
> suffered for years and years the
> greatest injustice at the hands of un-
> scrupulous money lenders. Till the
> Morrison outbreak, the hostility of
> the people did not show itself. He is
> the first to declare his enmity, and his
> friends and countrymen, who claim to
> have suffered the same as he, con-
> sider it their duty to stand by him.

It was in this growing spirit of camaraderie that the Scots and smaller community of French Canadians began to rally support around Donald Morrison. It began in a small way. Cutting by a settlement over by Red Mountain one evening Morrison stopped to ask for water and discovered a meal had been placed on the stoop. There was a note wishing him well and Godspeed. He ate heartily, cheered by the sudden realization that those who had despised him for his alleged crimes against the Duquettes had now found in his defiance of authority something admirable. Having eaten he moved on, knowing the constables might not be far behind.

For several days he stayed well clear of Megantic, positive in his own mind that the resentment built up against him there would not have softened as it had elsewhere. But late one evening he knew he must find out for himself the feelings of his own village. He walked boldly in through the front door of Pope's American House and ordered himself a drink at the bar. Suddenly the crowded room hushed and all eyes swung his way. His heart skipped a beat as he picked up the glass and took a swallow, then brought the glass slowly down to the bar. He had been too brash, he thought to himself, his mind racing to find a way out of this dilemma. For an agonizing moment no one moved. Suddenly he heard the scraping of a chair off to his right. Boots moved along the oak floor just beyond his vision. He waited, looking straight ahead as someone came up beside him. A voice told the barman to give him two more and Morrison's face broke into a grin. "*De man a tha sibh*, Murdo Beaton?" he said, greeting him. He heard Beaton curse him happily as the entire room swarmed forward to shake his hand. Beaton in the meantime pushed his way through the bedlam and stood by the front door, keeping a wary eye out for any stray constables.

He need not have worried. Morrison stayed an hour and left without incident. The local constabulary did not take the search for Morrison very seriously, partly because of frustration, partly because they didn't have their hearts in it. Questioning Scots on Morrison's whereabouts only led to false leads, and most took the hunt as a day's happy outing, when it didn't rain.

Indeed, no one in Megantic had the heart for it, that is, until Lucius "Jack" Warren decided he was just man enough to bring in Morrison.

Warren, an American, thought of himself as an adventurer. He liked others to think so too. Over the years he'd done a great number of wild things, though he was still on the happy side of thirty, and had somehow survived them all. The state police in both Maine and Vermont probably wished he hadn't, for he had caused them plenty of trouble. The Canadian Pacific Railways was extending its line into Maine to meet the Maine Central at Mattawamkeag, but the work was grueling and slow, the country desolate and friendless. The construction workers, feeling the need for some sort of solace, found it in the forbidden jug of whiskey; forbidden because Maine was a dry state. Thus an enterprising whiskey runner could have a thirsty market at his fingertips, as long as he didn't get caught.

Jack Warren was known to be one of the runners. And it wasn't surprising for him to end up in Megantic from time to time as he did again shortly after warrants were finalized for Morrison's arrest. It was here he picked up his "supplies" before heading back across the border for another run. He doubtless wouldn't have stayed in Megantic, either, had he not been intrigued by the news that an outlaw was roaming about, free as you please. That the police had yet to *spot* this fellow greatly amused Warren. He watched the local police going out on patrol. He observed the enmity stirred up between these men and the visiting handful of provincial police sent to "put an end to a ridiculous situation." With a little effort, he thought to himself, Morrison could be taken by the police's staying put, letting *him* come to them. Morrison, he knew by now, was brazen enough to show up anywhere.

Warren expressed such thoughts aloud one evening in the American House bar. Someone in the crowd expressed his thoughts aloud too; if Warren was so good, why didn't *he* capture Morrison? It had been a passing exchange of banter and yet all eyes turned toward the heavy-set American. Caught up in all the attention, Warren said he might lend a hand. He patted the revolver which was tucked into his waistband. After all, he'd seen this sort of action before.

This show of bravado brought a round of friendly cheers from the crowd. Emboldened, Warren added that it would take only one good gunman to capture Morrison; no need for bloodshed, either, if it were handled properly. Around the barroom the Scots suddenly went silent and sipped their drinks. The French Canadians present merely shrugged their shoulders. It was one minute to midnight, Saturday, the sixteenth of June.

By noon Monday word spread throughout the district that Justice of the Peace Joseph H. Morin from Sweetsburgh, in Missisquoi County, had sworn in the American Jack Warren as a special constable, giving him a warrant to arrest Donald Morrison. What had been an idle boast over beer on Saturday had become stark reality by Monday.

Just as quickly, Warren became Megantic's star attraction. He played his role with the shrewdness and cunning of a born actor. His revolver went from his trousers waistband to a holster on his hip, and by Tuesday he had started target practice behind Pope's hotel where he boarded. The racket of the exploding gun, with ammunition supplied by the authorities, continued most of the day, jangling more than a few nerves among the townsfolk. Many secretly hoped Warren might make a slip while perfecting his draw and accidently shoot off a toe—while others secretly prayed he might "slip a little higher."

The remainder of the week followed the same pattern—target practice and endless talk on how he, Warren, would capture "the outlaw." By Thursday his diatribe had worn thin, but he didn't let up. The townsfolk had heard enough. Besides, it was rather peculiar that Warren had yet to venture outside the village limits in his pursuit of Morrison. When confronted with this in the tavern, he said it was his plan to "stay put"; Morrison would eventually come to him. When the talk at the American

House became too boring for him, Warren moved across the street to Leet's or down the street to the Prince of Wales.

In the meantime, Donald Morrison moved about the country-side, keeping the local and provincial constables at a distance. He found food and lodging wherever he stopped and was on the move next morning before sunrise. He stayed clear of Megantic; he'd heard all he wanted to know about the boastful American called Warren. Morrison in no way wanted to gratify the man's ego by confronting him.

It had been a long dreary week for Morrison, and no less so for Annie MacDonald. An upstairs chambermaid working for the summer at the American House, Annie could only think of to-morrow, Saturday, June 23. It would be her first day off in three weeks and she felt she deserved it.

Monday had started off badly. She arrived at work suffering with the flu. But somehow, mostly with the help of her cousin and co-worker Marion McDermott, she had managed to drag her-self through the week.

Now it was Friday, Annie arrived at the hotel early, to finish work early. As she walked up the stairs to the third floor where she would begin cleaning rooms already vacated, she was shaken by the sounds of a barrage of bullets echoing down the alley and through the building. Annie clamped her hands tightly about her ears. It was the Yankee Warren again with his target practicing. Hadn't word gone around the hotel Thursday that he'd be away from Megantic today? He had boasted that if Morrison wasn't coming to him, he'd have to go to Morrison! Maybe it was too early for him to leave. Either way, if he didn't give up that racket, she would go down and personally strangle him with her very own bare hands.

Meanwhile Donald Morrison lay back on the sandy shore of Lake Megantic five miles away, soaking his feet in the water. It hadn't warmed up any, he thought, as he shifted his buttocks into a more comfortable position. This didn't help either, for now something was digging into his ribs and he reached down to dis-engage the irritant, his Colt revolver.

Donald pulled the gun free from the waistband of his wool

trousers and balanced it neatly across his stomach. He then un-
buttoned his dirt-stained shirt and leaned back again. Putting his
hands up under his head, he closed his eyes and felt the sun's
heat sliding across his face and chest. Relaxation was in short
supply these days, and he was in no hurry to arrive in Megantic.
Noon would be time enough, for by then the Warren fellow
would have gone away. Word had reached him that the American intended to come out to look for him, providing Morrison
with the opportunity to slip into town to pick up some needed
supplies and see some friends. With these thoughts drifting
around in his mind, he fell asleep. When he awoke it was almost
two o'clock, Friday afternoon, June 22, 1888.

Nelson Leet stood on the veranda of his hotel, directly across
from the rival American House, tugging at his worn watch chain.
One of these days, he thought, the chain would snap just as the
watch cleared his vest pocket and that would be the end of it.
Well, never mind, he murmured, holding the watch at arm's
length. It looked to be about two-thirty, half an hour before
things really got busy again inside. And half an hour's rest
sounded delightful, so he promptly dropped his overweight body
into his favorite rocking chair and sat back to watch Megantic
come to life after a long Friday lunch hour.

Maple Street was once more bustling with shoppers, wagons,
and small children. Mothers were filing in and out of Graham's
store next door, chattering and scolding and carrying on about
the price of food. Youngsters pranced in the street, seeing who
could raise up the most dust, all the while managing to dodge
the passing carts and horses. Leet watched, bemused, as their
mothers yelled at them from the safety of the wooden sidewalk,
loath to step into the street except as a last resort.

Among the many folk enjoying the hot afternoon sun was
George C. Mayo, a customs official from Maine who had arrived
in Megantic early this morning on business. At the moment he
was heading for the town hall. Quite suddenly, though, he
changed his mind, turned abruptly, and collided head on with
George Rodrigue, a farmer from Three Lakes.

Leet witnessed the amusing scene and the exchange of apolo-
gies which followed, then with a sigh worked himself out of his

rocking chair. A short walk would do him more good than sitting around on his posterior. Thus he stepped down onto the sidewalk and, nodding pleasantly at a few familiar faces, started off toward the lake on one of his familiar routes. It took him briefly through the park and onto the dock where he allowed himself a pause before turning back. When he reached his chair once more, he found he was sharing the veranda with François Thivierge, a local farmer who had undoubtedly forsaken the now-rowdy bar behind them for the relative quiet of the porch. Yes, Leet could hear that Warren fellow shouting louder than the others and knew that from then on it would be a busy afternoon and evening. Warren must have changed his mind about leaving town for a day or two in search of Donald Morrison. It was a safer move, Leet mused to himself, for Warren. The racket from the bar inside convinced him to stay out here somewhat longer today. Already it was five minutes to three.

Looking up he saw Antoine Roy step out of his blacksmith shop a few doors down, his face matching the blackness of his shirt, chest, and arms. Soon his brother Eustache Roy would join him and Leet would watch the pair heading for Pope's American House. He'd give them three minutes. With this he laughed to himself, then caught a movement out of the corner of his eye. Across the way, on Pope's balcony, the door had opened and two girls stepped out, both as pretty as pictures.

Nelson Leet recognized them as Annie MacDonald and Marion McDermott. He watched them playfully poking each other as they tiptoed toward the balcony railing to see what was going on below. Leet grunted, thinking that if that new hotel matron caught them they would be in for it, though they seemed oblivious to everything but their own enjoyment. That is how it should be at their age, he whispered to himself. If life . . .

But Leet's musings were cut short, for Annie was pointing excitedly up the street, leaving him wondering what had happened. Quickly, he glanced in the direction the girls were looking, but he could see nothing out of the ordinary. The street was filled with horses, buggies, and pedestrians and nothing seemed amiss. Surely . . . suddenly the hotel owner felt a chill strike him like a blow from a hammer, catching him in the midsection, then diffusing itself up through his torso and down through his legs. For among the crowd he spied a man walking far down the wooden sidewalk who looked decidedly like Donald Morrison.

Leet couldn't believe it. He closed his eyes. Age was playing tricks on him. But when he opened them the image of Morrison persisted, walking toward the American House. Leet gasped and jerked himself half out of the chair just as a voice beside him said, "Is that Morrison?" Leet froze. He didn't need to see the person beside him to know the voice was Jack Warren's. "Well, is it?" Warren shouted, his tone belligerent. Leet coughed and heard his own raspy answer as he sank back down into the rocking chair.

Jack Warren placed a reassuring hand on his hip as he stepped off the veranda. *Morrison, Morrison, Morrison*—the sound of the name rang in his ears. Stepping across the planked walk and onto the street, he could feel his body moving forward as though he were walking on air. His brain, numbed by the realization that *this* was Donald Morrison, refused to keep pace with his body. Someone had come into the Leet's barroom moments ago, whispering that Morrison was coming down the street. The crowd had roared with laughter, thinking it all a joke. Warren tried to laugh it off, but inside his stomach wrenched tight and he slowly withdrew from the room to find himself standing beside old Leet. Now, almost in the middle of the street, Warren felt a wave of nausea sweep over him. He was barely conscious of the sounds of scrambling feet behind him on the sidewalk.

Walking diagonally toward the corner of Pope's hotel, Warren found that the periphery of his vision seemed to have expanded. Without his glancing either way, movements on both sides of him were in sharp focus. To his right he saw people crowding the doorway of Matheson's store and to his left a small knot of them stood frozen to the road in odd poses, as though they were caught up in some kind of children's game.

Right then Jack Warren wanted to laugh out loud. Or *was* he laughing? His expression seemed to have a will of its own. Around him now these pasteboard figures were in motion, ducking for anything which afforded cover; jamming empty doorways, dropping behind an old water trough, plunging up alleyways. Then, miraculously, the entire village was hushed and the only sound of movement came from Morrison thirty feet away. As the distance between the men narrowed, Warren noticed Morrison slowing his pace, and for a brief moment he once more wanted to chuckle: Morrison, he could see plainly, wasn't as large as he thought.

Behind Warren, Nelson Leet remained transfixed in his chair. He knew he might be in danger, being so close, but his muscles had knotted and he couldn't move. He sat fascinated as he watched Warren reach the far side of the street. Morrison, just beyond, was carrying a small stick. He jumped the ditch, and it appeared as though he might walk around his adversary. Then they stopped, about eight to ten feet apart, as far as Leet could see. He didn't like this. It seemed so unreal, like a play going into rehearsal. And his body gave an involuntary shudder.

On the balcony directly above the two men, Marion McDermott clutched her cousin tightly. Annie, caught in a trance, leaned forward, shifting them both almost off balance, her eyes wide with excitement. Below them no one moved, except for a dog across the way, who idly sniffed at the corner of a building in search of a good spot to relieve himself.

Donald Morrison's breath caught in his throat. Warren, he cursed to himself. Damn him. Why was he here? He wasn't *supposed* to be here. They had said he wouldn't be. Then why . . . ? God *damn* them. Don't panic, he told himself. Look him over carefully. Funny, from what he'd heard, Warren was smaller than this. Warren was speaking. Morrison's mind skipped and jumped and came back to the moment. He had missed what he said. God damn it anyway. Why had this man gotten himself into this mess? It was for the locals to settle, not him. Anyway, he'd better try to avoid this Warren, before it was too late.

Morrison started to walk around him. Warren told him to stay where he was. Morrison said, "Stand clear," then repeated it several times. Warren ignored him.

Somewhere behind, Jack Warren heard a creaking noise, like a rocking chair. Or was it a shoe? Funny, he thought, he couldn't tell which. A puff of wind fluttered the ends of Morrison's mustache. Nerves, thought Warren unwisely. God *damn* him. In a moment it would all be over and he, Lucius Warren, would walk through the crowd and back into Leet's hotel. He had only had five beers, the last still unfinished. He could stand one right now, to moisten his throat. Yes, and what about a reward? Surely there was a reward for capturing an arsonist dead or alive. Dead, this one. Oh but Warren was thirsty.

Morrison stood stock still watching the other man's hand drop downward. He saw the glint of a revolver barrel clearing the holster. Before he knew it the muzzle was coming up fast. For one terrifying moment Donald Morrison was totally unaware of his own reflexes.

From the balcony above, Annie MacDonald caught Morrison's blurred reaction. Desperately she jerked herself forward. but Marion, clinging to her in sheer panic, pulled her back. At this precise moment Annie heard the single savage "*crack*" of a discharged revolver and she screamed with all her strength.

Across the street Leet's breathing came in one short, sharp intake of air. He saw Morrison's Colt explode, and for one crazy moment he thought the gun itself had blown apart. His eyes now swung toward Warren whose mouth was dropping open as his head flung back. For a second or two Jack Warren hung there, his twisted face laughing at the sky. Very slowly now his knees gave way and his torso pitched forward, his right hand still thrust out before him clutching his gun. Then the body went suddenly loose and fell as if lowered by puppet strings, and when it hit the dirt, quite dead, a wisp of dust rose from the street. His gun, knocked free by the impact, skidded a few feet and stopped and lay there, as motionless as the body near it.

No one moved. Seconds ticked by before the arm holding the other revolver retracted and shoved the smoking weapon back behind the waistband. Donald Morrison then moved forward as people around him came back to life. He bent down, looked at the crumpled form, then drew back. On the balcony above two girls slowly released each other, as tears, triggered by shock, cascaded down their faces.

On his hotel porch across the street, Nelson Leet sat trancelike, his forefinger and thumb methodically kneading his thin gold watch chain. All at once he saw the town come alive; people were charging forward. Leet stirred, his watery eyes following the stumbling form of Albert Pope as he rushed down the

Donald Morrison about the time of his trial in 1889. He was in his early thirties when the photo was taken.

Canadian Pacific Railway locomotive the Countess of Dufferin as she looked in 1883 at the time of Donald Morrison's return to Megantic, Quebec, from the West. (Photo, Canadian Pacific)

A typical colonist coach. (Photo, Canadian Pacific)

The Duquette farm on Ness Hill, formerly the property of the Morrison family, after the stable was burned in May 1888. Lake Megantic is in the background with Megantic Mountain beyond. (Photo, J. P. Jones)

The village of Megantic around the time of the story. The arrow points to the American House, in front of which Donald Morrison shot and killed Lucius "Jack" Warren on June 22, 1888.

Pierre Leroyer, guide and *coureur de bois,* one of the two captors of Donald Morrison. He is seen here with his pet moose. (Photo, J. A. Jones)

Peter Spanyaardt (with mustache) of the Montreal *Star,* who covered the Morrison hunt and subsequent trial. (Photo, Montreal Star-Canada Wide)

steps to drop beside the body. A second man was bending down too.

Within seconds a crowd enveloped the scene, ten deep, and as Leet watched them he let his attention settle on Morrison, who stood motionless among them. Suddenly Leet wanted to jump up and run to Morrison and tell him over and over that he knew it was in self-defense that he used his revolver; he wanted to tell him how he saw Warren's gun coming up even before Morrison dropped his stick. But Leet couldn't *get* up; his muscles were disobeying him as they so often did when getting out of bed in the morning. He struggled now and failed, and with all the tension inside him his vision suddenly went out of focus as tears filled his eyes. And he wept silently to himself, his mind ajumble with thoughts of all the malice and misunderstanding, frustrations and accusations, which had come together and culminated in the death of a man whose boasts were bigger than his sense of what was real and what was not. Jack Warren was dead. Later Leet would find the man's beer glass on the bar only half finished.

THREE

OUTLAW

7

WARRANT FOR MURDER

June–August 1888

The gunfight which ended in the death of Lucius "Jack" Warren struck no one harder than old Murdo Morrison. It left him grieving for his son and blaming himself for the shooting. If he and Sophia hadn't been so uncompromising with Donald, this never would have happened.

In all his seventy-six years Murdo had never been a demonstrative man, and Warren's death only caused him to withdraw further inward. Sophia, sensing his hurt, tried her best to comfort him; he would not respond. Murdo fast became a recluse, working on an old sewing machine in a darkened corner of the small log cabin near Marsden and producing vests and coats and other wearing apparel for his wife. A glimmer of life returned with the periodic visits from Donald after the shooting. Their son took great risks in visiting them at all. He was wanted for murder and the reward for his capture had climbed to $2,000.

Sophia Morrison's belief in her son's innocence went unquestioned. She knew him to be a deeply committed man—an aggressive person perhaps, but not vindictive. She never put her feelings into words, yet she expressed them clearly through her defiant struggle to keep the family intact.

Sophia was to place much hope in the assurance that the Scottish community would not turn its back on a young man whose only goal was to achieve dignity among his own kind, a dignity not only for himself, but for them too. Her judgment was in no way misplaced. She saw and heard a quiet ground swell growing in support of her son, the recriminations for his alleged attacks on the farmer Duquette forgotten. She now had only to wait for the situation to straighten itself out, as she knew it would. She had only to wait for Donald's infrequent visits and to comfort her increasingly withdrawn husband.

On the day of the shooting Donald Morrison had eased himself back through the knot of curious onlookers who gathered about Warren's fallen body and walked away from the village of Megantic as unhurried as he had arrived, but little question remained that he now was truly a man on the run.

Later that Friday afternoon Morrison sat on the shore west of Sandy Bay and stroked the goat, then ruffled its chin where the long tuft of coarse hair began. The goat, the sole companion of Lemieux the hermit, lowered its head and gently butted itself against Morrison's shoulder in a friendly gesture of welcome. Finally he frolicked off down the beach, leaving Morrison alone to watch Lemieux working on his small boat. Neither spoke. Lemieux never would talk to anyone nor did Morrison have the inclination. However, he kept a wary eye out for any suspicious movement from the woods or along the shoreline.

Though he had much on his mind, Donald Morrison tried to keep any thought of Warren a thing of the past. He was dead; nothing could bring him back to life. Besides, such was the life of a bounty hunter; Lucius Warren had been nothing more. He had also been the aggressor, forcing Morrison's hand by going for his revolver without even identifying himself. During all his years out West, Donald Morrison had killed no one and he had always made certain he was never a target. Today in Megantic he *had* been a target and he had pulled out his Colt and fired in self-defense. His only problem now was staying alive, and he remained here, near Lemieux and the caves, to learn what would happen next. He knew that many who had helped him evade the law before the shooting of Warren would never consciously support the same man if he was wanted for murder.

Malcom Matheson, a tall, angular man with a heavy dark beard, pulled the door of his general store shut behind him, bent down to give the key a sharp twist, then turned to survey Maple Street as he dropped the heavy key into his pocket. The sounds of laughter and murmuring voices from the American House—a barometer for the mood of the village as a whole—had returned to normal, following an afternoon which had been nothing short of chaos. A murder in the main street wasn't a daily happening in Megantic, and an argument arose over what should be done about the body, what with Dr. Millette's whereabouts unknown, the undertaker having no authority to remove it, and the police not yet arrived.

Matheson had kept clear of it all. In the turmoil which followed the shooting he caught up to Morrison as he was moving through the crowd and told him to head for Sandy Bay. Morrison nodded; Matheson could find him there. Matheson patted him on the shoulder, then turned away.

Back in his store following his moment with Morrison, Matheson went directly to his small office, closed the door, removed his black hat, and pondered what should be done next. Warren's death was far from his mind as he tried to devise some sort of plan which would keep Donald Morrison free, at least for the moment. He wondered at the same time how much help the community would be now.

Within a few minutes the storekeeper knew what he must do, though time was running short. Rumors in the village were circulating that police had already been summoned from Sherbrooke, Montreal and the Quebec detachment of the Provincial Police to help track down the killer. Essentially, what Morrison needed was friends about him whom he could trust. It would be an easy temptation for someone to go after a reward, which would surely be posted, by letting the police know Donald's whereabouts. Such an opportunity must not arise.

Sitting down at his desk, Matheson listed every person who knew Donald Morrison well. From this he finally selected six, with a possible seventh, whose support would be unwavering. The list started with Hugh Leonard of Stornoway (a small community to the northwest of Megantic), a close friend of the Morrison family, who had known Donald all his life. Next, Finlay McLeod, hotel owner, and Malcolm McLean, postmaster, both of Spring Hill, followed by another trusted friend, John Hamilton, a millwright from Winslow, a few miles northeast of

Stornoway. From the North Hill area, way to the west, came Angus McLeod and John Hammond from Lingwick.

Matheson added Murdo Beaton's name to the list, though he wasn't sure if the lad was in Megantic or back in the Vermont quarries. He would inquire. In the meantime he took a moment to write each of the six giving them a brief account of the shooting and comments from a few who had actually seen it happen, including Nelson Leet who had assured the storekeeper that Donald shot in self-defense. Morrison must be kept away from the authorities, he wrote, at least until some sort of negotiations can be worked out. So far Donald Morrison had seen little evidence of "justice" and it would be up to each of them to ensure his safety.

He then described the "network" to be set up by what he called the "Morrison Defense Organization," which entailed each man in his area to keep track of the police and report their movements and to help Morrison move from area to area, providing him with food where possible. Each would have to visit other Scots in his area and seek their support, whether by leaving food for Morrison out on their porches or misleading the patrols with faulty information.

Finally, each would try to keep the others informed about what was happening in his district. He wasn't sure how many people in the communities would aid Morrison, but he'd bet it would be high. As a postscript, he said he'd try to visit them soon and further establish what tactics they might use.

With the shop closed and the letters duly mailed, Malcolm Matheson lingered for a few moments on Maple Street before walking down the lane to pick up his horse and buggy. Within an hour and a half he and the outlaw were walking together along the shore of Lake Megantic. A small, bright-eyed goat meandered along behind them as the storekeeper outlined his motives and identified the members of the Morrison Defense Organization. Morrison remained silent.

Peter Spanyaardt of the Montreal *Star* was a newspaperman's newspaperman: he loathed cranky editors who penciled his copy to shreds; he detested being sentenced to the rewrite desk, and to him accuracy should never interfere with a good story. By "accuracy," he'd explain, he meant such trivia as spelling proper names correctly or going so far as giving good grammar precedence over a quick and ready phrase.

Spanyaardt's major challenge in life was not merely *landing* a good out-of-town story, but rather keeping it alive so that he *remained* out of town. The reporter had been working on just such an assignment since the second week of June. He had received a tip from a lawyer friend in Sherbrooke about a girl murdered in Danville, in the Eastern Townships, and broached the idea of covering it with the Montreal *Star's* editor. The editor wasn't interested in any ordinary murder. Spanyaardt insisted it was no "ordinary" murder. The victim was a girl in the Salvation Army, Lily Powell by name, and the suspects, so far at large, were thought to be related to the victim. The editor glanced warily up at Spanyaardt's round mobile face, catching the wide-set twinkling eyes. As always, Spanyaardt stood with feet planted solidly on the floor, his plump body tipped forward as though ready to do battle. This reporter had a persuasive way about him and as the editor watched Spanyaardt waiting patiently for an answer, the editor couldn't help but admire the man. Yes, he told Spanyaardt, he should follow the story through.

Before leaving, Peter Spanyaardt had also mentioned a strange incident which occurred in the Megantic area. The editor, wise to the ways of reporters, gave Spanyaardt a sideways glance and listened while the reporter told him how some man was being sought by local police on a charge of arson and intent to kill. The editor wasn't about to be taken in this time. He asked if the man had burned the town down. Spanyaardt hesitated. No, but he'd burned down a stable and log house. And the second charge, only *intent* to kill? The reporter nodded, then explained that the community wasn't being very helpful in co-operating with his capture. . . . Spanyaardt's voice trailed off and the last words he heard were that he'd better stick to Lily Powell—it made better copy.

Spanyaardt, finding himself in Sherbrooke with a full hour on his hands before the train left for Danville, went directly to the office of his friend and lawyer, J. Sidney Broderick, who greeted him with genuine affection. Sidney Broderick was a handsome

man, with an expansive forehead topped by a slightly receding
hairline. Reputed to be one of the best lawyers in the Eastern
Townships, Broderick had always tempered the seriousness of
his profession with an abrupt sense of humor. He had also made
sure his friends were not drawn exclusively from legal affilia-
tions, but rather from a broad spectrum of life about him. He
had met Spanyaardt in a Montreal court while the latter was
covering one of his cases.

On this occasion, after telling each other how much *older*
they looked, Broderick gave him further information about Lily
Powell, though he admitted he hadn't much to add. The suspects,
so far on the loose, were possibly uncles of the dead girl and
their names were Fred Allen and Lewis Perkins. He then gave
Spanyaardt several contacts he might speak to in Danville.
Spanyaardt was delighted. He jotted down the names in his
notebook, then asked if the lawyer had heard anything about an
arsonist over around Megantic. Broderick shrugged as he leaned
back against his chair. He knew little, he said, other than that a
Scots family had lost their farm and it seemed the youngest son
had threatened to drive the new owner and his family away.
Quite mysteriously the stable had burned down, followed by the
house and there was talk of some shooting, but no one was in-
jured. Spanyaardt noted this, then looked up. Could he attach a
name to the family? Broderick shook his head, wondering aloud
why such a case had interested him.

It seemed to Broderick that it was an everyday case of arson,
with a little shooting on the side. Spanyaardt agreed, but he had
heard also that the Scots community wasn't being very co-operative in aiding the capture of the young man. Broderick had
heard it too, but the Scots were peace-loving people, he said,
who might not want to get involved. The reporter sighed. It
could be, but his intuition was itching. As they walked down to
the Sherbrooke railway station he asked Broderick to send him
word at the British American Hotel in Danville should anything
further develop in Megantic. Sidney Broderick's eyebrows went
up and he laughed out loud. How much was it worth to him, the
lawyer asked?

After several weeks in Danville Peter Spanyaardt's continuing
saga on the Lily Powell case was wearing a little thin. He had

milked the story from every possible angle and had now only to wait the capture of Perkins and Allen. In the meantime he had wired back short news reports he had dug up around the area, and when the suspects were actually caught, during the week of the eighteenth of June, Spanyaardt knew he would soon be heading back to fill in for the vacationing rewrite man, Randall.

Spanyaardt had written the last story on Lily, which saw the two men handcuffed and put aboard the train for Sherbrooke. They would await trial set for early August. It was Friday, June 22, and he toyed with the idea of spending the weekend in Danville, not having to report back to the editorial office till Monday.

Returning from the railway station after filing his roundup story, he was halfway across the hotel lobby when he heard his name called. A clerk behind the large reception desk was waving his arms in Spanyaardt's direction. Walking over, he was handed a telegram dated from Sherbrooke at 4 P.M. The first thing which crossed his mind was that Perkins and Allen had escaped. Opening it quickly, his eyes dropped to the signature: "Sid Broderick," then to the brief message above: MEGANTIC STORY NOW MURDER.

Spanyaardt hit the landing in full stride and within five minutes was back at the hotel desk anxious to pay his bill, when the clerk handed him a second telegram. Spanyaardt smiled. From Montreal. It would be from the editor, telling him to hurry down to Megantic. And that, he said to himself, was precisely where he'd been heading.

By nine o'clock Friday night Spanyaardt had filed a short news story about the killing from information he had obtained from the crown prosecutor's office in the Sherbrooke courthouse. A bad train connection had precluded sending the report from Megantic, but he would be there in the morning. The Saturday edition of the Montreal *Star* was to carry his brief and, as he was soon to learn, inaccurate story (the facts, he protested later, came directly from the crown prosecutor). The item was buried on page three:

QUEBEC, June 22—A cold-blooded murder was committed today at Lake

Megantic. A man named Morrison was obliged to fly from Sherbrooke to avoid arrest on a charge of arson. He took to the woods and was followed by Constable Warner [*sic*] some days ago. Nothing was heard of him until today when Attorney-General Turcotte received a telegram from Mr. Belanger, Crown Prosecutor, at Sherbrooke saying that Warner had come up with Morrison at Lake Megantic Corner, but in an attempt to arrest him was shot dead. Belanger asked that armed men be sent by special train to capture the murderer.

Lucius "Jack" Warren had died from a bullet which entered the neck, Dr. Millette concluded in his autopsy report. It had passed through a carotid artery and shattered the spinal column close to the base of the brain. Death was instantaneous. The authorities tried to find any next of kin. It was thought he was born in Charleston, Maine, but Maine state officials had no record of him, and when none was found, preparations were made for burial in the Echo Vale Cemetery, across from John "Boston" MacDonald's, on Monday, the twenty-fifth of June.

The day was wet and the service, conducted by a local Presbyterian minister, was short. On the outer fringe of the small, sodden crowd gathered at the grave stood members of the Morrison Defense Organization solemnly surrounding Donald Morrison and Augusta McIver. They had told him it was sheer lunacy to attend the funeral, but he insisted. He rebuked Augusta for wanting to be with him, but she took no notice. Thus they had all come, and as the final prayer gave way to the driving rain, the Defense Organization took its leave.

Meanwhile, the authorities were busily hunting him down. Word from government circles in Quebec insisted he be captured without further delay; the story of his defiance already bore overtones of police incompetence.

Within days police were everywhere, arriving by special

order from Sherbrooke, Montreal, and Quebec, and going about their task with enthusiasm. This vigor waned somewhat when they admitted, grudgingly, among themselves that it wasn't *one* man they were up against, but rather an entire community of Scots and French Canadians. Their every move was thwarted by false information about his whereabouts (dispensed in the most imaginative ways). The locals hid the outlaw in their very homes when the trail became exceedingly hot and kept the man alive by placing food out on back stoops for him at night. And there was always the clandestine Defense Organization, membership unknown, who traced the policemen's every move and led them a merry chase.

The police were not alone in their efforts to track down Morrison or the Defense Organization ringleaders. Upon his arrival in Megantic on June 23, Peter Spanyaardt had installed himself in the American House and sent back daily reports of interest. But he was most eager to cap it all with a first hand personal interview with Morrison himself. Indeed, his newspaper insisted on such a story.

He tried for four full weeks to make contact with Morrison or the Defense Organization, by moving about the hotels in an effort to become a familiar face, only to confront distrust in the community on one hand and in the police on the other. The latter didn't like the press nor reports that Morrison was still at large. Caught between the two, Spanyaardt found himself facing a third obstacle: his editor insisted he would be recalled if his stories didn't produce a new angle. Obviously, Spanyaardt would have to change his tactics, and if no one would come to him, then he'd *have* to win someone's confidence.

He had come to the conclusion that the owner of the general store, Malcolm Matheson, was linked with Morrison. Thus during his fifth week in Megantic he frequently dropped into Matheson's store to swap idle gossip. On the afternoon of Friday, July 27, he found himself alone with Matheson and finally mentioned his eagerness to meet Morrison and get the story in his own words. Spanyaardt said nothing else. Matheson didn't answer.

The following week the reporter set phase two of his plan

into operation. It was a rainy Sunday morning, the fifth of August, that he put together a definitive story about the outlaw, his background, and what had happened to Megantic since the shooting. He had hoped the outlaw might read the article and by chance be thus disposed to an interview. The reporter was desperate. He hoped that the newspaper would print it in its entirety. That evening he walked down Maple Street to the park. On his way back he dropped into the railway station and wired the story to Montreal. It appeared the next day—in full:

SPECIAL TO THE STAR

LAKE MEGANTIC, August 6—Things at Megantic are not half as bad as painted. Instead of a place where murder and incendiarism run riot and where every man parades the railway station with a shotgun to see whether there are detectives on the incoming train, a stranger arriving at the village finds a quiet little settlement beautifully located right at the foot of Lake Megantic, inhabited by apparently law-abiding people. Although a few days ago Morrison was hiding in the vicinity of the settlement, he has never shown himself in the place itself. Lately he had removed further into the country.

It was good so far, he thought, his eyes dropping down through the copy.

The arrival of six Government detectives, big fellows, would make spendid targets for Morrison's six shooters. And should any of them succeed in killing Morrison, their lives would not be worth a farthing, and as things stand now I am quite sure that nothing less than a regiment of soldiers

could effect his arrest, and only at the
expense of considerable bloodshed.

Reading on, Peter Spanyaardt realized again that he wasn't
about to establish any closer ties with the police. He had
weighed this carefully while writing the story and come to the
conclusion that they hadn't been much help in the first place.

Further down the story mentioned the Scots' feeling toward
such local papers as the Sherbrooke *Gazette*, which, they said,
"continually misrepresented Morrison while favoring his ene-
mies." Morrison's friends had taken a singular position that they
would not allow him to be taken alive, or themselves either,
should they be caught defending him. Spanyaardt went further
by identifying Matheson only as "a gentleman of education who
owns considerable property in the neighborhood" in his quote:

> "We do not approve of Morrison's
> conduct, but we thoroughly believe
> that the boy has been badly treated
> and we simply want to see him have
> fair play which he cannot obtain till
> his side of the story has been pub-
> lished in the public press."

Spanyaardt was to stay awake late into the night, reading the
article over and over and before he finally dozed off, fully
clothed on the bed. He knew the item told the story with hon-
esty. If it did nothing to gain him access to Donald Morrison,
then so be it. Nevertheless he had written it as he'd seen it, here
in Megantic.

The small deserted house near Galson was cut off from the
road by a heavy stand of birch and maple trees, thus eliminating
a view of the open country and rolling hills beyond. Donald
Morrison had known of the spot, abandoned several years ago by
a Scots family who had moved West, leaving the wood-frame
house and its barns to rot and crumble. Morrison had located it
easily enough and moved in, at least for the moment. He might
soon move on, but there were things which needed doing, even if
the others didn't particularly agree.

Among the dissenters was Malcolm Matheson, who now paced the small porch shaking his head, his hands shoved deep into his pockets. Moments before he had given Donald a long, detailed account of the impossibility of setting up a meeting with the Montreal reporter. Without doubt he'd be followed. The police were following *anything* that moved these days; particulary anything that *moved out of town*. It was far too dangerous for another reason: the Defense Organization was proving itself useful, but it wasn't organized well enough to pinpoint every step the police made and the interview could put his friends in jeopardy. Already police patrols were popping up where least expected, Matheson added, his hands waving in the general direction of the countryside. He stopped long enough to glance at Murdo Beaton and Augusta, who were both leaning against the railing. In short, Matheson continued, a meeting with Spanyaardt would be out of the question.

From the look on Donald's face it was obvious he didn't share Malcolm Matheson's view. Augusta was pleased, but said nothing. She watched Donald bring a hand up to stroke the mustache, then drop his hand to the railing and pick up the newspaper. It was today's early edition of the *Star* which Augusta had brought with her. Donald opened it and in the fading light read Spanyaardt's article once more. Then he turned to Matheson, his finger jabbing the paper, almost shouting as he quoted the piece ostensibly spoken by the "gentleman of education." When he finished he looked at Matheson, letting a smile spread across his face. Matheson tried to smother a grin behind his massive beard, but didn't succeed. He sighed and shook his head while Donald, jubilant over this small victory, began planning how to get Spanyaardt safely to Galson.

Murdo Beaton now entered the conversation. Before he went home he would stop at Kenneth Nicholson's and John Buchanan's at North Hill to see if they were available. He paused and looked at Morrison, his eyes sparkling against his faded blue shirt. How many men would they need? Donald rubbed his face with his hands. About twenty. They looked at Matheson. He agreed. Twenty at least. They would have to be posted at intervals along the road almost back to Megantic. Maybe twenty-five, some with families too, he said. Donald looked at Augusta and grinned. Eight or ten from Lingwick, Red Mountain, and North Hill, including William MacDonald and his sons Dan and Robert. And from the other direction, the Leonards from Stornoway, Finlay McLeod and Malcolm McLean from Spring Hill. The list grew as the plan took shape. Finally Malcolm Matheson leaned back against the post and in his quiet manner suggested they pick a date. Morrison grinned broadly. Tomorrow night, he said.

The remark brought a modest cheer from Murdo Beaton and Augusta. She stepped forward, her hands clenched with inner vitality. It had to be done on the spur of the moment, she said, her voice strong and even. Catch the police off guard. Should they get a mere whiff of some liaison between Spanyaardt and Donald they'd break their necks keeping on his trail. Donald looked at her proudly, but Malcolm Matheson's smile was grim. The storekeeper shoved a hand into his vest pocket and extracted a small briar pipe, saying he still wasn't in favor and he knew others would find it too risky but . . . He glanced up. They'd best get on with it, hadn't they?

On Tuesday morning, August 7, Peter Spanyaardt awoke, rubbed his eyes, and looked about the small hotel room which was flooded with sunshine. With one motion he swung his pajamaed legs over the side of the bed and sat up. The one thought which had kept him awake half the night was that *something* had to break today. One more "noninterview" story and he'd be hauled back so fast his head would spin. With this in mind he pulled himself off the bed and within ten minutes was shaved, dressed, and out in the fresh air for his daily walk to the lake and back.

Still well before seven, he walked into the small hotel dining room with the previous night's Montreal *Star* tucked under his arm. He chose the same table by the window, ordered his usual plate of eggs and bacon, then opened the newspaper. He had decided earlier to corner Matheson directly after breakfast, show him the news story and demand an interview. He'd even *plead* if necessary, saying that coverage would end abruptly if he wasn't given access to Morrison. He would also remind the storekeeper that the *Star* was the only newspaper with a full-time reporter covering the story. Without results his editor would summarily pull him back to Montreal, with little doubt. Now, as he waited somewhat impatiently for his eggs and bacon, his eye caught a small heading in the column next to his Megantic story. Date-lined Sherbrooke, it proclaimed, ALLEN AND PERKINS ACQUITTED. The body of the story told how the pair involved in the "Lily Powell mystery" had been found not guilty. He'd keep an eye on it, he thought, the moment his breakfast arrived.

He was wondering who else might have killed her when he looked up to find Malcolm Matheson approaching. Marvelous, he said to himself, thinking he would get his little speech over now instead of later in the store, but before he could summon the words, he was told to be on the 7:30 train for Sherbrooke this *morning* and to get off at the first flag stop. All was arranged. Spanyaardt's mouth was agape. He watched the tall Scotsman turn and walk deliberately from the dining room. Peter Span-yaardt had no hunger for the plate of eggs and bacon before him.

He arrived at the Megantic station with only seconds to spare. He was unable to hurry because he knew the police were beginning to take him seriously and already several pair of eyes were watching him as he boarded the train. Moments later he was staring through the mud-spattered window as the coach tilted to one side taking the first bend leading from the village to head down the tracks toward Marsden.

No sooner had the train gained speed than it immediately began to slow. Spanyaardt, standing on the open stoop, swung his body free from the moving car and hit the gravel at the run. Then, catching his balance, he waved up at the conductor who in turn reached for the signal cord to assure the engineer up front there was no reason to come to a full stop.

Spanyaardt found himself staring at the Echo Vale station. He was alone. He waited, wondering if this were the right place. A man appeared at the far end of the platform. He came Spanyaardt's way and as they passed, he told the reporter to fol-low him. The latter obliged and crossed the tracks to drop down along a small path which meandered through the woods, eventu-ally ending on a lonely stretch of road near Sandy Bay. He was told to wait. He did so—for more than two hours.

During this time he saw no one. They probably didn't trust him, he thought, and obviously they weren't taking chances.

By eleven Spanyaardt figured something had gone wrong or that whatever plans had been made were now scrapped. Funnily enough, Matheson hadn't even mentioned anything about a meeting with Morrison; Spanyaardt was merely going on the premise this was the mission. But why out here for more than two hours? He . . .

The sound of an approaching buggy caught his ear. He could hear the clinking of the harness and the grinding of the wheels against the broken road as it came closer, though the sounds, echoing off the surrounding woods, made it impossible to locate the direction from which the buggy was approaching. Then he saw the ears, the head, and the body of the horse as it came up over a rise and dipped down into the small valley to meet him. Sitting alone in the buggy, stiff and expressionless, was Malcolm Matheson.

Giving the reporter a perfunctory nod, Matheson slipped the reins under a thigh and with both hands opened his dark coat. Pushed into his waistband were two "bulldog" police revolvers, of sizable persuasion. He watched the reporter's reaction, then said crustily, "There is still time to turn back." Spanyaardt shrugged and calmly pulled himself up beside the storekeeper, then settled back against the stiff leather seat. Looking down he noticed a Winchester rifle and a loaded cartridge belt at his feet. Matheson was taking the reins and with a quick upswing of the hands brought them down gently on the horse's back, which set the buggy into motion.

They had gone less than a mile when the storekeeper informed the reporter that their mission was highly dangerous. He'd been against it from the first because it could bring great peril not only to Morrison, but to all those involved. "I tell you plainly," he added, his voice close to a growl, "if there should be any treachery on your part, neither of us will come back alive. And should any of the detectives try to follow us, and after fair warning persist in their course, I will shoot them down rather than have my family disgraced." For a moment there was silence as the gravity of the moment sunk deep into Spanyaardt. But there was no turning back. He looked at Matheson, saw the flicker of the blue eyes and felt the intense emotion simmering in this likable Scotsman. Then he nodded for a second time. "I understand," he said.

Peter Spanyaardt was lost for most of the long buggy ride. This was his first excursion beyond the boundaries of Megantic. He realized they had traveled generally in a northwesterly direction and at some time during the morning they had passed close to Spring Hill, though their winding, twisting route kept them rigidly on the back roads. It might have been an arduous trip had not Matheson been such an enjoyable companion. Once the ground rules were agreed to he turned out to be an entertaining conversationalist. He told the reporter how he had arrived in Megantic after opening stores in Stornoway and Lennoxville. He had also been in the lumber business, he said with a modest grin, but then who *hadn't*. Later his talk of Highland folklore held Spanyaardt fascinated as they plodded across the countryside.

Beyond Spring Hill the land sloped to the left. Spanyaardt could feel the pitch of the buggy rather than see it, for the woods drew up close, leaving only enough room to pass. Soon, however, the road struck a long high ridge which carried them free from the surrounding forest. Now the land on both sides, particularly to the west, moved down and away like a carpet of patchwork green as it dipped down into the valley and struggled up the far side to be stopped dead by an uneven stretch of blue horizon.

Though the view held his attention, Peter Spanyaardt became increasingly aware of the people along this desolate section of road. Since the other side of Spring Hill he had noticed men, women, and children busily gathering fungus or wild roots, chopping down trees, or merely resting by the roadside. At first he thought nothing of it, then it struck him that some sort of signal was being exchanged between them and Matheson. Although not positive, the reporter waited until a man appeared ahead with a shotgun, looking every bit like a farmer out hunting. However, as the buggy drew alongside, Spanyaardt caught a glimpse of expression on Matheson's face which denoted some sort of questioning. This was returned by an almost imperceptible nod from the man with the shotgun. From this moment Spanyaardt knew he was in the center of a well-conceived lookout system which could summon in no time a horde of Scotsmen to one particular spot.

For what seemed hours the buggy bumped along, swinging left onto one road, then right at the next, until at last the ridge too was behind them and the road flattened and veered toward a clutch of buildings half a mile away.

The buildings turned out to be Stornoway, a once impressive village which years before had seemed destined to be a commercial center for the region. Then the railway came and took a more southerly route through Marsden and Spring Hill. So Stornoway remained forlornly sedate in its own way, with a few shops and houses and a large, ornate two-story structure called Leonard's Hotel.

It was behind the hotel that the horse and buggy were stowed away, in the driving shed, while Matheson and Spanyaardt were taken inside for lunch. Their appearance caused a flurry, and after introductions were made, the travelers were made comfortable. Lunch followed a drink, at which time Spanyaardt was to learn several things of interest. First, the stopover would be brief, Matheson said, and secondly, their journey was almost over.

Spanyaardt found the Leonard family to be of strong Scottish stock. They had gained a reputation for being shrewd tradesmen and would have been leaders in the district had the railway not scuttled their plans. Hugh Leonard had remained to become the mayor of Stornoway however, and James, his brother, had taken over operation of the hotel. A third, younger, brother, John, had taken to law and opened a practice in Sherbrooke.

During the meal Spanyaardt was also to learn about Duquette. The French Canadian was on his list for an interview, but as yet he hadn't managed to track him down. Hugh Leonard nodded as he wiped a napkin across his lips. Though he had no confirmation, he heard Duquette had quit the farm on Ness Hill, selling it to a man named Ferrier Chartier. Matheson, sitting on the other side of the table, confirmed the rumor: the sale price was $700. And where did Duquette go finally? Matheson thought he had purchased a smaller farm closer to town, but he didn't know where.

To Spanyaardt, anxious to make the stopover brief, Malcolm

Matheson showed a disarmingly annoying habit of delaying the event. First he reported their horse was lame, a small stone having worked its way painfully up into the creature's hoof. No sooner had this been taken care of than the buggy developed a bad spring or problems with the wheel; all of which led Peter Spanyaardt to wonder if his meeting with Morrison was about to be, or indeed *had* been, abandoned. But having no vote in the matter, he made himself comfortable and took to his notebook. It wasn't until late afternoon that Matheson led him outside to the waiting buggy and they were on their way.

They headed southwest, Spanyaardt believed, in the direction of Tolsta. For the past week he had all but slept on a map of the area and if his memory served him correctly Tolsta would be somewhere ahead.

Within an hour, the village of Tolsta was behind them and, as before, Spanyaardt noted the lookouts posted at intervals along the route. No longer, however, were there women and children to be seen, but rather well-armed men whose dispositions were markedly different from those of this morning. Every few minutes men stepped boldly from the woods and appeared to speak angrily to Matheson in a language the reporter did not understand but took for Gaelic. It didn't need translation: these men were displeased with seeing a stranger. Matheson's expression didn't change as he drove on.

Spanyaardt had been a good passenger. Though stiff and sore and unused to such travel he good-naturedly had suffered every bump and jolt in silence until he could take it no more. Needing a moment to get down and stretch, he turned to Matheson just as the buggy swung to the right and entered a small road. The reporter grunted and looked ahead.

A moment later he saw a small house through the trees and behind it several barns. The buggy stopped before the house. A small boy, about five years old, appeared on the porch, grinned, and ran back inside. Matheson got down, mumbled something Spanyaardt couldn't understand and stepped toward the house, leaving his companion alone in the rig.

Less than five minutes had gone by when the door opened; Matheson was waving and as Spanyaardt stepped down his aching legs almost gave out from under him. Anxiously now he climbed the three steps and entered the house and was ushered into a dimly lit parlor. He waited, hearing voices. One was a woman's voice, but he couldn't make out what they were saying. He was about to sit down on one of the few chairs in the sparsely furnished room when the door behind opened and he turned to find himself standing face to face with Donald Morrison.

Spanyaardt was to note later: "I can remember the thrill that went through me, and also how I unconsciously looked at his trousers to see if his murderous revolvers were in his pockets. His hands were free, and he stretched out his hand with the cordial words, 'I am Morrison, how are you?'

"For a moment I was nervous; it was the first time I had shaken hands with a man who, outside regular warfare, had killed another, but the confident and hearty handshake he gave me immediately established a sort of bond between us, and the interview went as easily as falling off a log."

Spanyaardt could hardly believe that at last he was in the same room with Morrison. He quickly searched for his cigars, offered one, then waited. He found he wasn't obliged to ask many questions, at least at first, "for he walked up and down, acting out the whole tragedy of that fatal meeting over again," while the reporter wrote quickly in his notebook. During a pause he described the outlaw as a "tall, gaunt, big-framed Scotchman, with a ruddy complexion and steel-blue eyes, high cheekbones, tawny moustache and a rather serious mien, which however was lightened at times by a specially charming smile."

The interview was going well, though Spanyaardt still had a great deal of information he wanted covered. When he had the chance, he asked Morrison about the farm and how he lost it, posing a question which he thought might bring the interview to an end. It had to be answered. Taking a deep breath he said, "Someone shot through Duquette's window and fired his stable and house. Was that you?"

Spanyaardt watched the eyes harden, the head swinging his way, the mouth drawn across the teeth. "No," said Morrison, "it was not. I did not do the shooting and can prove that during the burning of the stable I was in Spring Hill, and the burning of the house, in Hampton."

A pause sent Spanyaardt scribbling down the words, anxious to quote Morrison exactly. The other man, sensing the urgency, waited patiently. The reporter finally looked up again. "Did you ever think of giving yourself up?"

Morrison turned to the window. "When the matter goes through the press," he said calmly, "so that people can see what the trouble is, I will know better what to do. I have sent a letter to Major McAulay asking for the $900 which he wrongfully deprived me of, being willing to let his law costs stand against mine. If he will return this money I am ready to leave the country . . . and never return."

"Do . . . do you intend shooting anyone?"

Morrison's head swung around. "No, I don't intend to kill anyone and I hope to God Almighty I don't have to." Then he turned back to the window and looked out at the darkness beyond. The interview had ended. Spanyaardt stood up as Morrison came back toward him, his hand extended. "You have my story," he said with obvious emotion, "and you are the only one I have spoken to freely. Be . . . just, that is all I ask." They shook hands once more and at the door Morrison glanced back. "I think I can trust you."

When the early Wednesday morning train bound for Sherbrooke pulled out of the Megantic station, Peter Spanyaardt was aboard writing the finishing touches to his interview with Donald Morrison. He could not trust sending it from Megantic, and though he hadn't had sleep for more than twenty-four hours, he knew he wouldn't close his eyes until the story was wired safe and sound from Sherbrooke. With any luck, it would make the final edition of today's Montreal *Star*. He did better than "hope"; he prayed. And as the train cleared the bend and whistled through Echo Vale, his eyes dropped to his lead paragraph for the fortieth time.

> LAKE MEGANTIC, Que., August 8— Morrison was interviewed by me yesterday. The difficulties I encountered before I could see the man who had defied the law so long were innumerable. But I was not to be undaunted [sic] and after considerable hunting among Morrison's friends . . .

8

CATCH IF CATCH CAN

AUTUMN 1888—FEBRUARY 1889

By early fall the Honorable Honoré Mercier, Quebec's effusive premier, was fit to be tied. The "Morrison" business had been going on for more than three months and the opposition was taking the government to task at every damnable opportunity. *Three months* Morrison'd been on the loose, and if the attorney general didn't *end* this ridiculous chase, he, Mercier, would raise more than just hell.

Nothing ruffled Attorney General Turcotte, not even this latest outburst. He quietly lowered himself into one of the premier's more comfortable chairs, lit a cigarette, and answered with characteristic bluntness. Morrison was elusive, he said without emotion. Even with extra constables sent from Quebec to affect the arrest, the situation was far from satisfactory.

Mercier was not amused. Wire services were already carrying the "continuing saga" of Donald Morrison from coast to coast, and they had the effrontery to make the authorities appear as the villains. And didn't Turcotte read the Montreal *Star*'s latest interview with the outlaw? *Mon Dieu*, Morrison had his nerve! No, Turcotte would have to work out some sort of truce with Morrison. At least they might talk to the man and learn what he had to say. Obviously he couldn't be allowed to go free, but a truce might bring the situation to a head.

By the twelfth of October, a Friday, the Morrison Defense Organization made arrangements with the authorities to bring Donald safely to Sherbrooke. Here, before going to Quebec to stand trial, he would sign a guarantee never to molest Major McAulay. For their part, officials promised that the reward money would be used to pay the outlaw's defense. When Mercier heard these details, he was delighted.

He wasn't so delighted by Monday, October 15, when the Defense Organization, on Morrison's behalf, said the trap was closing prematurely without concrete assurance that the reward money would be turned over to them. The authorities should prove their sincerity, members of the organization said. Besides, none of them thought it fair that Malcolm McAulay should get away scot-free.

Mercier fumed. Couldn't the police merely *talk* to Morrison personally? The answer was an abrupt, "no," which didn't rest easily with the fiery premier. Summoning Turcotte once more, he ordered him to *flood* the Eastern Townships with police, bounty hunters, adventurers, *anybody* who might corner the outlaw—now wanted dead or alive.

Turcotte mentally counted how many more provincial police he could spare, then suggested thirty. Mercier thought it piddling few. Didn't his attorney general have any better ideas? Turcotte nodded wisely. They could dispatch the Army, he said. Premier Mercier broke into laughter. Send the Army to capture one man? No, they would have to think of another way. Had Turcotte considered hiring private detectives, such as Pinkerton's? Turcotte shrugged. He hadn't, but he would look into the cost per man. Mercier agreed, then came around his desk and clapped a friendly hand on the attorney general's shoulder. While the attorney general looked after that side of it, Mercier said, he would drop a personal letter to Montreal's Mayor Vital Grenier about the possibility of sending some of his city police to Megantic. He had already talked to Police Chief George A. Hughes, who thought the idea might be "open for discussion."

By November the approach of winter came in gusts of chilly winds and temperatures which dropped nightly below the freezing point, and though the authorities laughed at the suggestion that Donald Morrison might still be at large by Christmas, they admitted no one had come within sight of the outlaw. At least they didn't *think* so.

Among those bent on capturing Morrison, none was more harried than George Hughes, chief of the Montreal Police Force, who would neither confirm or deny to the press that some of Montreal's policemen were "holidaying" down in the Eastern Townships—at the expense of Montreal taxpayers. This pressure, building over the weeks, finally forced the robust police chief to schedule a press conference for Tuesday, December 4. And the moment he arrived, he knew his day wouldn't be one of his better ones. A Mrs. Scott, of the Woman's Christian Temperance Union, had somehow managed to slip undetected upstairs and parked herself outside his office, refusing to move until she had a moment alone with the chief. His defenses were down; he invited her in.

Mrs. Scott was a matronly, good-looking woman, who directed life about her as though in command of an army regiment. She ordered Hughes to sit down, then launched an attack against Montreal in general, and Chief Hughes in particular. Couldn't he *see* the city going to pieces around him? When he paused to reflect, she took it as a defensive tactic and countered with a strong offense. Striding to his desk, she leaned forward and dropped her voice. Did the chief of police know music was being played *illegally* in one of the drinking establishments on Rue des Commissioners? She had heard it yesterday with her very ears. From the street, of course. *Music*, she said, which contravened the liquor act. And what would it lead to next? Chief Hughes nodded wisely. Quite true, he said, catching her completely unaware. He would back her up too, the moment she and a witness entered the tavern and lodged a formal complaint.

For the second time in as many days Mrs. Scott of the WCTU couldn't believe her ears. She go *into* a tavern? This isn't what she wanted, she cried, her emotions getting the better of her; she wanted action, she wanted *arrests*. On this note she burst into tears and ran from his office, leaving Chief Hughes only minutes away from his dreaded press conference.

"Chief Hughes made a clean breast of his connection with the Morrison affair," stated the news report in the late edition of the Montreal *Star*. He openly admitted permitting some of his best detectives to go to the Eastern Townships in search of the outlaw.

"My connection with this business," he said, "commenced on September eighth, when I received a letter from the Honorable Mr. Turcotte asking me if it were true I was willing to undertake the capture of Morrison, if the government was prepared to give me one thousand dollars."

Asked what his reply had been, he added, "I answered that such was not the case. But on September twentieth I received another letter from the attorney general authorizing me to send a sufficient number of men to affect [sic] the arrest and forwarding me $500 to cover expenses. Part of this amount was employed in sending out reliable men to discover the means to be taken to secure the outlaw. My men . . . reported to me and I sent a private report to the attorney general. I informed him that the only means to arrest the alleged murderer was to go with a band of determined men and arrest anyone who interfered. . . ."

The press conference ended after a few more details were aired. Chief Hughes excused himself before the reporters began poking into things which he didn't want poked into. For one, he had given the impression that his "detectives" had merely gone down to find ways of affecting the capture, then file a report, which in turn would, at Hughes's pleasure, be sent on to the premier of Quebec. None of the press had asked if any Montreal police had *remained* there to help round up the outlaw. It was a good thing they hadn't.

Winter was not kind to Donald Morrison. He could go nowhere without leaving telltale tracks in the snow, especially in areas where the only marks besides his snowshoes were made by animals. Winter however gave him one concession—a reunion with an old friend.

Having spent the night of December 10 in a rough cabin up from Ayres' sugarbush, he had gone to the stream to break the ice and wash. A movement from behind brought him lunging sideways as he struggled to free his Colt from the confines of his heavy coat and scarf. All at once he let out a whoop and leapt to his feet. Not thirty paces away Norman MacAulay was leaning forward on a horse calling him every name he could think of.

Donald had reached him by the third epithet and dragged him
bodily off the saddle. They hit the ground, rolling over and over,
clouting each other until they were breathless. Then they sat in
the snow, Donald watching the old sly, reckless grin of his
friend spilling across his tanned face. Norman threw himself
back in the snow chanting, "Outlaw, outlaw, outlaw, you old
bugger."

And it was *true*, he said, true as he was sitting in the snow.
What *else* had brought him back East but word that his friend
had killed a man with his Colt and now there was a price on his
head. Norman stopped and looked at Donald. He hadn't come
back to collect the *reward*, hell no, but to see the famous outlaw
for himself.

Donald laughed and wandered back to the stream, rubbing
his bewhiskered chin. Norman watched as he broke the inch-
thick ice with his boot heel and washed his face without removing the scarf about his neck. To be sure he'd heard about Donald
clear out to Calgary. It was in all the newspapers, so he came
home to make sure his friend wasn't going strange in the head.
For the life of him, he couldn't envision Donald as an outlaw.
Himself maybe yes, but not Donald. He came back East knowing Donald wouldn't be capable of keeping himself out free of
the law without him there to direct operations. They laughed as
Donald dried his face with the end of his scarf, and they set out
looking for Augusta.

It was almost Christmas. The three were to see a great deal of
each other, though the McIvers didn't take too kindly to their
daughter's association with a known criminal. Talk was getting
around . . . they told her, but she turned away, knowing it
couldn't last forever; even now police were lodged down at
McLeod's Hotel in Spring Hill keeping a special eye on her.

By Christmas the Quebec provincial police assigned to the
Morrison case were still deeply annoyed by interference of the
Montreal detectives who had arrived unceremoniously a month
before "to find better ways of effecting the arrest of Morrison."
They were not here, it seemed, to take part in the actual hunt,
only here to report their findings. It had made for bad feelings
all the way around. Working at Christmastime wasn't much to

their liking either, and unofficially the search found few police out beating the bushes for the outlaw, thus affording Donald Morrison time with his mother and father in Marsden and a meal with his brother Murdo, Marion, and their children on their farm across the way from the old Morrison place. Christmas had softened a number of hearts.

With the coming of the new year, 1889, Augusta McIver faced the reality of Donald's future with a new sense of direction. She knew he would have to go away. Nothing else was left, and she took the opportunity during Donald's absence with his family to conspire with Norman MacAulay. He had hinted several times that he would soon be heading West and she suggested he might consider taking Donald back with him. It was considered, unofficially, of course, that the authorities might pursue Donald no further than the provincial boundaries, should he decide to take himself westward, thus solving the matter for everyone concerned.

Norman's face broke into a smile. He had confided this in no one, he said, but the moment he heard about the shooting on June 22, 1888, he came East, admittedly a little later than he had hoped, with the express purpose of persuading his friend to quit the Eastern Townships. He flushed and took Augusta's hand. The West, he told her, held a great future for Donald and herself, if only they could persuade him to leave. It was her turn to blush. She hadn't thought of it in terms of her and Donald going West and she quickly changed the subject. Hadn't Norman noticed how Donald had changed? Norman nodded. The old humor was gone, and he had grown a stubborn streak as long as a tapeworm. Donald still clung to the hope that he would be vindicated and that he'd live to see the day when Major McAulay was brought to task for his dishonesty.

For two days the old friends roamed the countryside talking about old times on the cattle drives. Nothing much had changed out West, Norman ventured, but Donald smiled and said if Norman nurtured any thoughts of getting him back there, he should forget it. If he left now, this business would plague him the rest of his life. He couldn't run from it and he'd be damned if he

CATCH IF CATCH CAN 91

would go to jail for something that wasn't his doing. No, he'd
stay and fight.

Norman MacAulay said good-by three days later—and rode
out of his life. Augusta McIver knew she might not be far behind. In saying good-by.

With the holiday season over and a new year in the making,
the search for Donald Morrison intensified. Fifty provincial
policemen, plus a handful of militia, were sent down from
Quebec. Use of the Army, though sparingly, was an experiment
which Attorney General Turcotte insisted upon. Law and order,
he told Premier Mercier, had to be maintained in other parts of
the province and the better the situation if a few soldiers could
fill in for the police. Mercier knit his brows over this little ploy,
but he also saw its necessity. Let the opposition find out, he
warned Turcotte, and there would be an uproar.

With the arrival of reinforcements, bringing the search party
to more than one hundred persons, the authorities decided they
needed better control over "project outlaw." Patrols, used hap-
hazardly in the past, would be marshaled like an army maneuver,
reports would be filed, troop movements logged and tallied.
The Prince of Wales Hotel on Megantic's main street became
central headquarters, with all information being sifted through
it. The whereabouts of every man, every patrol, must be known
at all times, with regular reports sent back from a patrol "in
the field." If Morrison was spotted in one area, an emergency
patrol would be dispatched to back the other up. Substations
were also established, one in Lingwick and a second in Stornoway, with a few men left permanently at Spring Hill. The search
began in earnest.

For its part, the Morrison Defense Organization merely tightened its collective belt. With subleaders in every community,
those involved had only to report "troop" movements to these
men and continue to harass the searchers as best they could by
withholding information or sending them off on wrong pursuits.
Donald Morrison solved one particular problem which bothered
him—his leaving snowshoe prints in the snow. Often he would
cover miles of territory, leaving behind a solitary trail which

could be followed by the most amateur tracker. He suggested members of the Defense Organization might take the odd "walk" about their territory, if only for the sake of exercise, which would serve as a good distraction. The tracks should indicate only one person and be made particularly after a heavy snowstorm, when fresh snow was the most telltale time for Donald to get about.

The scheme worked well. Police headquarters in the two-story Prince of Wales got many an excited report from patrols indicating they were surely closing in on Morrison, having him cornered in the woods. The emergency patrol would be dispatched in haste, only to find them trailing an old Scot who said he had grown weary of remaining indoors all winter.

Not to be outdone, the police devised a new stratagem: sudden house-to-house searches, which would widen to encompass an entire community.

One of the first areas to come under close scrutiny was North Hill, beyond Gould. In the second week of January, word reached the Prince of Wales Hotel that Morrison had been seen there for several days. Several patrols were dispatched at once.

Morrison had indeed gone up to North Hill, and though he could seldom be found in one spot for more than a day or two, the festive season had put him in a happy mood; he lingered longer than was prudent with the McRitchie family, old friends who lived there.

Morrison had always shared a fine sense of camaraderie with the McRitchies, particularly with their sons John and Donald. They were a sly, quick-witted pair in their late teens whose careless bravado and nerve he admired. Together the three already had had several narrow escapes from the police, but nothing as perilous as what faced them on the tenth of January.

It was late that morning when Morrison took his leave, thanking the McRitchies for their kind hospitality. Mrs. McRitchie gave him a sudden spontaneous embrace and watched him running through the snow to the barn with her son John, who had offered him a ride to Gould. Morrison didn't want to put the lad in any danger, but John laughed it off, insisting the fresh air would do him good. Soon the horse was hitched to the sleigh and they left the driveway at a gallop.

They had no sooner turned off the North Hill road when they saw a large sleigh with a team of horses coming toward them. Although still some distance off, John McRitchie suddenly hauled on the reins, which sent the spirited horse back on its haunches. The sleigh, John said was filled with policemen—he'd seen it before. With terror rising in his throat, John looked wildly about him to see if this sleigh might turn around in the narrow road. It couldn't. The snow had drifted in, leaving a space barely wide enough for one sleigh. His mind numbed with excitement, he glanced at Morrison who sat beside him urging him to keep going.

Slapping the reins, John McRitchie braced himself as the sleigh pulled ahead, then gave the reins to his companion. Morrison's puzzled look was now greeted with a McRitchie smile. He was to drive on, he told the outlaw, and exchange places with him as quickly as possible, thus putting Morrison on the outside, away from the other sleigh. With seventy-five yards of wind-blown snow between them, Morrison shifted over, then pulled down his hat, pushed up his muffler and waited for the worst.

As the team approached, Morrison pressed his boots hard against the wood frame. The reins felt good in his hands as he shortened his grip, should they need a hasty exit.

The other sleigh was close now. Morrison tapped the horse gently, guiding him to the right to leave as much space as possible for the larger sleigh to maneuver. Out of the corner of his eye he counted the policemen, giving up when he reached ten. Their faces were bound in thick gray mufflers, leaving a mere slit for the eyes, and they wore fur caps which tied beneath the chins. Each had been issued heavy greatcoats which reached down to their knees. They sat like leaden statues propped against the wind.

Both drivers pulled their sleighs deep into adjacent snow-drifts, to give themselves room to pass. This forced the outside runners up into the snowdrifts, leaving the sleighs angling inward.

Donald felt cold sweat breaking out on his wool-capped forehead. Making a clucking sound with his tongue, he urged his horse forward as the driver of the larger carryall did likewise with his team. Being inexperienced, the man drove the team too deep into the snow and, sensing panic in the horses, yanked on the left rein to bring them down closer to the center of the road. Morrison and McRitchie, directly opposite the carryall, saw the danger in the move before the other driver had. He too learned fast enough, for in swinging the horses away from the snowdrift, the front runners swung through forty-five degrees, forcing the body of the carryall over into a perilous angle.

Aboard, the policemen groaned in unison as they hastily tried shifting their weight right to the high side. Donald, on the other hand, wasn't about to be crushed by the carryall should it tip, apart from the possibility of being showered with policemen. Quickly he snapped the reins at his horse sending the animal skittering ahead. At this precise moment John McRitchie leapt free of the smaller sleigh, hit the snow and rolled to his feet. With a bound, he slammed his body against the low side of the carryall, screaming at the man with the reins to drive the team *straight ahead* and not to the left.

With a creak and a groan the sleigh jerked forward, stopped and moved again as the horses strained against the traces. Then it came free, first plowing deep into the snow, then swinging into the narrow track.

Back in the smaller sleigh, Morrison's wide grin was hidden behind his own frosted muffler. He gave the policeman a hearty wave while mumbling under his breath for McRitchie to quit shaking hands and quit repeating, "It was nothing, nothing at all," so they could get the hell out of there.

The winter of 1888–89 seemed endless. The searchers scoured the frozen countryside looking for some evidence that the outlaw was still around. Many of them wouldn't have recognized him if he'd joined them for a drink in the Prince of Wales in Megantic. His photographs were distributed among the policemen, though now he wore a beard and didn't particularly resemble his photo. In fact, he had just had a scolding in Spring Hill over his appearance. Teasingly, Augusta had told him a shave and bath would do marvels for his morale, even if it couldn't improve his appearance. He had taken her abuse goodheartedly and was leaving by way of the back of her garden when the front yard turned into a melee of shouts and jostling lanterns. Policemen were running about and pounding in the front door. Morrison waited in the safety of the woods awhile, lest the police overstay their welcome.

The system set up by the Morrison Defense Organization worked, on the whole, like a finely tuned watch. An evening never went by that Donald didn't find food awaiting him on some back stoop. He'd often eat immediately or carry it off to a nearby barn, where he would make himself comfortable for the night. Seldom did he stay in homes because he didn't wish to cause trouble should the house be searched—with him in it. People watched for him, passing on messages from other communities when he appeared. Often he would hear of raids in the planning stage. Drinks in the Megantic taverns loosened a few tongues among the police, and when an area was to be hit, Morrison would move on.

In theory, the Defense Organization felt they could carry on forever. In practice, the best laid plans often went awry—like the fuss at old William MacDonald's in North Hill.

It was a blustery day in late January, several days after the search at the McIvers' home in Spring Hill, when the Stornoway patrol strayed beyond its boundaries and struck with force at MacDonald's home in North Hill. With their rifles at the ready the police and militia crowded through the front door and spilled into the hallway, only to find themselves confronting a teen-aged Danny MacDonald, who stood his ground on the stairway aiming a revolver in their general direction. The sight of such a young lad defending the household brought chuckles from the constables, but they kept their distance while assuring him they had come to do no harm.

Danny MacDonald wouldn't have any of it. The gun trembled in his hands as he told them outright that this was the second time in a week that their home had been singled out by a search party, and with his father unwell, the whole business was most upsetting. He inadvertently showed them how upsetting it was by waving the pistol in great wide circles and even once closed his eyes. The policemen would have run for cover, if they hadn't been jammed so in the narrow hallway. They told him to calm down and apologized, admitting it wasn't at all fair to cause such a commotion at this time of night.

By this time Danny had kept the police long enough for his older brother, Robert, to run to the barn and bring back a ladder, propped it up to the second floor window, and hasten Morrison's escape. Danny delayed the police a few minutes longer, lest they take their leave and see someone bounding into the woods, by saying he wondered why anyone would bother harboring an outlaw when it could only get them into trouble. The police were pleased, Danny was pleased. They left, tumbled into the carryall and headed for Gould. They had no sooner swung out onto the road when Morrison was back, sure the police like lightning, wouldn't strike twice. At least, not in one evening.

Like all families in the district, the MacDonalds had become fair target for the roaming police patrols. No one took offense; the sound of the front door being wrenched off its hinges hardly turned a head, after the umpteenth visit. The only worry it caused the family was what to do about William MacDonald. A steadfast, dour old Scot, and an elder at the local Presbyterian church, the family feared him to be too honest a soul to lie should the authorities ask him pointblank for Morrison. Old MacDonald did not agree. He proclaimed before his family that he stood by his Scottish principles and would betray no one, even if faced with such questioning. He never had to put his conviction to the test. Whenever the police were suspected of being within half a mile of the farmhouse, the old man found himself unwittingly locked in the barn or stable or, more often as not, in the outside convenience.

If the Scottish communities found humor in such happenings, the authorities did not. The police grumbled about the cold and the forced marches in the middle of the night, which netted them not so much as a glimpse of Donald Morrison. Local constables took exception to the overbearing conduct of the provincial police and went about their work halfheartedly—or less, if they could get away with it. Often they did. Morale dipped, patrols cut their circuits short, and the hotels in Megantic did a good business among the visitors. By the end of January it would have been difficult to find anyone who gave a damn about hunting down Morrison.

The Honorable Honoré Mercier was the exception. He could feel the malaise setting in clear over to the parliament buildings in Quebec. Morrison had been on the loose for eight months now. *Eight months,* he said, bringing his fist down hard on his marble-topped desk. It was quite incredible that one man should remain free, with a veritable small army hounding him all over the countryside. Yes, yes, he knew about the bloody Scots blithely abetting him at every turn, he said, looking over at his attorney general. It was still just one man, running against a whole regiment which bellyached if asked to pursue him on foot.

Attorney General Turcotte drew deeply on his cigarette, held the smoke in momentarily, then exhaled, watching it distort the premier's features beyond. When he spoke, he did so with complete control. All he could do now was deploy more men. After all, if the *army* couldn't track down Morrison *in the snow,* then more men would be needed to blanket the area. Blanket it with soldiers as deep as the snow itself . . . !

Mercier was in no mood to dicker about the number of men he needed, and he said so. He was about to emphasize the point by bringing his fist down on the desk, thought better of it, and locked his hands behind his back. No, he said, more men wasn't what was needed. What was needed, he said, moving slowly out from behind the desk, was a general. A leader. Someone who could think on his feet, match wits with Morrison and his band of ragamuffins. Outwit them at every turn. *Mon Dieu, that's* what was lacking.

Turcotte eased himself deeper into the chair. A general? he asked. Who did the premier have in mind?

Premier Mercier's face broke into a smile. Not a *general* per se, he said, but rather a leader. Maybe a judge, with a shrewd sense of command.

A judge? asked Turcotte.

A *judge,* snapped Mercier, looking pleased with himself.

FOUR

THE CHASE

9

THE NEW REGIME

FEBRUARY–APRIL 1889

Callite Aimée Dugas, judge of the sessions and extradition commissioner, was a man of stern countenance, the indelible consequence of his chosen profession. He looked, at times, like an oversized gnome, with his round face highlighted by thick eyebrows and deep-set eyes. His hair, thinning at the crown, had been a source of minor irritation to him since his midthirties, but he prolonged the agony of baldness by wearing it long on the sides and grooming it up and over the top of his head.

Premier Mercier had picked the Montreal judge as the best possible person to conduct a manhunt. He knew him as a man of extraordinary energies. He was tough, shrewd, and took on his assignments with a tenacity that shamed younger men. Dugas would handle the Morrison affair as if nothing else mattered.

The opportunity of leading an expeditionary force into the Eastern Townships intrigued Aimée Dugas. Passionate in the art of stratagem, countermaneuvers, and barefisted wits, Dugas' imagination was fired by the prospect of a manhunt, no matter what the odds. The judge readily accepted the offer and immediately began assembling his team.

These he chose as scrupulously as chess pieces, matching and discarding until the exact combination fell into place. It was late

February. Dugas hoped the actual preparation for the expedition would take less than a month.

For his second-in-command he chose Adolphe Bissonette, high constable of the courts in the district of Montreal. He might at first have seemed out of place in sophisticated company, for he was a slow, ponderous man whose dogged determination would balance any flightiness shown by other members of the group. Though not known for a sense of humor, Bissonette showed flashes of shrewdness when least expected.

Judge Dugas also needed someone who could be intimidating without giving way to violence. He could find no one better in this category than Silas H. Carpenter, the tall, aggressive chief of the Montreal Police Detective Bureau. Dugas knew Carpenter to be ruthless and yet personable enough when it suited his purpose. In reality, he was a man who held himself apart and liked it that way. He accepted the Morrison case with a quick, nervous nod.

Constable James McMahon, a six-foot two-inch giant of a man, was Dugas' third choice. Associated with the Montreal Police Force since his midteens, he had built a modest reputation as someone whose fearlessness was matched only by his forthright nature. McMahon was lean for his size, indisputably tough, and it was widely known that whenever the detective bureau found itself in a particulary ticklish spot, he would bail them out. He had an intuitive sense when tracking down leads that others had long given up. Constable McMahon wasn't without his foibles, however. He had worked diligently for the force over the years, and at age thirty-three he hungered for a promotion that had always eluded him. The Morrison expedition seemed to offer the chance he'd been waiting for and he swore to himself it would be his leg up the police ladder.

At last Dugas was ready. All the members of the team had been chosen. The pieces were all in their place, at least on the judge's side of the chessboard. Each now was eager to enter the game.

Life for Donald Morrison that February was anything but orderly. Not the least unsettling was Augusta's tearful decision to leave the Eastern Townships. Torn between her love for Donald and loyalty to her family she finally gave in to their wishes and prepared to leave for Boston.

Pressure from her parents and friends had become too much, she told Donald, as she cried in his arms, and now she was too worn out, mentally and physically, to resist them any longer. If she didn't get away, at least for a while, she would break down altogether.

Donald wept inside, but he found no words to comfort her as she sobbed into the night. He could offer her nothing and knew her leaving would bring relief to them both. For weeks he had watched the color draining from her face, her eyes go haggard and begin to sink deeper behind dark circles. She had lost the happy, whimsical way which used to sustain them both when life seemed hardly worth the bother. No, he couldn't see being without her, but to watch her waste away was even more unbearable. And they loved and they parted.

C. B. Allardice of the *Star* was leisurely climbing the stone steps of the Montreal city hall when he heard a noise which seemed alien to its surroundings: gunfire. Being a reporter with a better-than-average sense of news, he investigated the source of this noise with a thoroughness which left behind him a wake of unhappy city officials. They were more unhappy when they saw the afternoon newspaper of March 27.

POLICE PEPPERING

Anyone visiting the [Montreal] city hall this morning and hearing the continuous bang! bang! bang! of carbines being discharged at the target in the cellar would suppose that the police are preparing either to quell some impending riot or to march to the front to repel a foreign invader. All morning the carbines were being examined in preparation for a trip to the [Eastern Townships] concerning the Morrison affair.

If gathering these facts in the basement came with apparent ease, not so was his reception upstairs.

> In police circles everyone is 'mum' about the affair. The Chief [Hughes] himself said he knew nothing . . . and didn't seem over-pleased when he said that much.

Allardice also tracked down Judge Dugas who, it seemed, wanted to use the press to clear up any misunderstanding about his role in the Morrison case.

> He [Dugas] wished it stated that he goes to Megantic simply as magistrate to bring to justice, if possible, Morrison and his abettors and that in as quiet a way as possible, with the ordinary legal proceedings.

Some questions had also been raised the next day about Dugas, who also prided himself as the lieutenant colonel of the 65th Regiment, a local militia unit, smuggling some regular army chaps along with his expedition. Allardice, who had always got more from a blunt frontal attack, put this question to the judge who answered, somewhat startled, "This is not a military expedition. I shall take with me the high constable and a posse of men. I shall not take anyone out of the 65th or any other regiment."

Allardice wasn't finished. "I suppose," he said offhandedly, "several of the city detectives will go with you . . ."

Dugas wasn't pleased. Neither was he about to become embroiled in local politics. His answer was candid. "I would rather you would not say anything about how I am going and with whom I am going. I shall simply go out to Megantic and do my duty." The interview was over.

Preparation for this expedition into the Eastern Townships had taken Dugas a month. Gathering the men and equipment and taking care of travel, food, and board left him annoyed and impatient. Finally, on Friday morning, March 29, the expedition left by rail for the Eastern Townships.

Setting up his headquarters in the Prince of Wales Hotel in

Megantic, Judge Dugas wasted no time deploying his troops. Though the party didn't arrive in Megantic until after eleven o'clock Friday night, by ten o'clock Saturday morning, the thirtieth of March, men were hastily dispatched to posts throughout the communities.

Dugas' plan was to establish base camps, manned by reliable men, in strategic spots. This had been done previously, on a limited basis, though not to the same extent nor with the same determination. Police who had already spent months on the search for Donald Morrison found their new leader a hard taskmaster.

First to be posted were McMahon and Carpenter who set up a camp of sorts outside Marsden, across the way from Murdo and Sophia Morrison's log house. Dugas reasoned that Donald Morrison would likely as not make periodic visits to his aging parents, and he wanted a permanent force there when he did, even if it meant literally camping out in tents.

Included in the Montreal detachment was Sergeant Leggatt, who was to command those already billeted at McLeod's Hotel in Spring Hill. Others took up posts at Stornoway and at Gould. Remaining at headquarters in Megantic, along with two auxiliary forces, was the Dugas team of Sergeant Clarke of the Montreal Police, expedition doctor J. G. Tremblay, who was also the official clerk, and High Constable Bissonette. The net was spread now, its corners pegged securely, and Judge Dugas was ready for the big catch.

The Morrison Defense Organization heaved a collective groan, knowing that at last war had been officially declared. Malcolm Matheson welcomed the new surge of enthusiasm among the police because he and Morrison agreed they had been taking too much for granted lately, their wariness dulled by poor performance on the part of the searchers. Morrison knew only too well he had become far too cocky and he had more than one close escape to prove it.

The previous week he had set out from Galson to Red Mountain and, suddenly tiring of the cross-country trek, taken the connecting road, though he knew it to be an unwise move. The traveling was easier and besides he hadn't seen a bluecoat for three or four days. His spirits too were down to rock bottom, with the

departure first of Norman MacAulay, then Augusta. Those days
following her leaving had left him remorseful and almost on the
verge of giving himself up. He might well have done so had not
Murdo Beaton and Malcolm Matheson convinced him to hold
on; a new man would be taking over the police force, and rumors were he might make an honest approach at negotiations.
Donald had agreed and he'd been heading north to Red Mountain to keep clear of the main centers of activity.

As he trudged along pacing one snowshoe after the other, the
cold wind snapping at his clothes, his mind blurred with images
of Augusta and Norman and the enjoyment they had found together for so short a time, he finally glanced up to see half a
dozen leg-weary policemen coming around a bend not fifty yards
ahead.

With no chance of escape, he pushed ahead, whistling loudly
to the wind and drifting snow until he stopped before them,
waving his hands about his body and remarking how blasted
cold it was. The police, ill-humored to the man, nodded in
unison and were bidding him good day, when one of their company peered closer at the muffled figure, asking incredulously if
he were one Donald Morrison. Donald laughed uproariously,
taking it all in good fun and saying if he *were* the outlaw, would
he now be standing there conversing as if they had all stepped
out of church? The officer's eyes narrowed to slits between muffler and fur cap, while his mates roared approval at the young
man's wit and shouted that they'd best be off to Galson before
this damnable weather brought them to their knees.

The officer pulled back, bringing the flat of his mitt across his
eyes. He nodded at Morrison, then joined his men who had
wished the young man *"Beannachd leibn"* (good-by) and had already started down the road. The look on the stranger's face
remained with the officer for many hours, and in the morning,
when reporting the extent of his patrol the previous night, he
was told to keep a sharp eye peeled for the outlaw; he had last
been seen near Red Mountain.

For Morrison the incident had proved one important fact: if
he truly wanted to be captured, he need only carry on as halfheartedly as he had been lately. Thus he welcomed the news
that the police had drawn the battle lines and the fight would

begin in earnest. The Defense Organization, he told Matheson, would have its hands full, if only a quarter of what he heard about Judge Dugas was true.

If anyone felt cut adrift from the current goings-on, it would have been Peter Spanyaardt. Under Dugas' new decentralization policy, rumors kept breaking from one side of the Eastern Townships to the other. Morrison seen near Megantic Mountain; Morrison traced in a barn near Weedon. Spanyaardt was here in the Townships to report the capture of Donald Morrison and nothing short of a report from the scene would be accepted by the newspaper. This left Spanyaardt not only confused but exceedingly fatigued. In desperation, he finally wired the Montreal *Star* from Megantic that it was next to impossible to follow up three or four different leads at the same time. Couldn't the *Star* spare one more reporter? The newspaper left the request hanging for a few days, then realized from the amount of copy Spanyaardt was sending, he might well drop from exhaustion. The editor belatedly dispatched C. B. Allardice to the rescue, a reporter already familiar with Dugas and his expedition.

Spanyaardt and Allardice divided the territory, with Allardice settling himself in at the hotel in Marsden. Here he could keep a close watch on Chief Detective Carpenter and Constable McMahon and the western portion of the area, which included Scotstown and Bury and northward to North Hill, Red Mountain, and Gould. When Carpenter and McMahon moved, Allardice would follow. Spanyaardt then would remain essentially in Megantic, with forays to Stornoway, Tolsta, Galson, and Spring Hill. If anything broke, each would inform the other immediately.

Meanwhile Judge Aimée Dugas wasn't about to wage war sitting on his posterior in Megantic's Prince of Wales Hotel. Although he had only arrived the night before (Friday, March 29), by Saturday afternoon he had already ordered a large sleigh to be brought to the steps of the hotel. Warned that it might be colder outdoors than he imagined, the judge cast the suggestion aside and strode bold and bareheaded onto Maple Street. Whoever had made the suggestion about it being a trifle cold knew what he was talking about. Dugas eyed Bissonette who was wrapped, and all but lost, in his huge buffalo coat. Telling his party to wait, the judge went down, then subsequently up, the street in search of a fur hat, wool gloves, long one-piece underwear (he would have settled for any size, he told Tremblay later), and heavy boots. He found none of these items. Every store was inconveniently out of stock of everything he wanted. Undaunted, the judge went back to his hotel, put on all the clothes he owned, then returned to the waiting sleigh.

Soon the party was crossing the ice on Lake Megantic in the large blue Beauce carryall, pulled by a husky team of matching Percheron draft horses. Dugas, still hatless, had strategically placed himself between Bissonette on his left whose bulk deflected the wind sweeping in across the open lake from the southwest, and Sergeant Clarke on his right. Spanyaardt in the front seat beside the driver and behind Dr. Tremblay shared the rear seat with a Captain Giroux of the 65th Regiment, and the lawyer McLean from Sherbrooke, the man who had so badly counseled Donald Morrison. McLean's obvious switch in sides had angered not a few Scots, Murdo Beaton among them. Peter Spanyaardt's invitation to join the party had come as quite a surprise; it seemed Dugas was making an effort to patch up any bad feelings with the press.

By the time the sleigh reached shore at Sandy Bay, the party was frozen. Spring Hill wasn't far, the driver, a crusty Scot, said from deep inside his own warm wraps, and within the hour Dugas and Co. were stamping their feet and rubbing the circulation back into their arms before the crackling stove in McLeod's Hotel. They had been greeted by the half-dozen police who had arrived earlier under the direction of Sergeant Leggatt, replacing the few who had seen duty here. Dugas announced that after lunch they would head immediately for Stornoway.

Finlay McLeod was a subdued host. He wasn't enchanted with having police under his roof, though the choice was not his. Besides, he disliked Dugas from the moment he saw him, though the emotion he felt was one of fear rather than hate. Dugas looked like a man who would stop at nothing to achieve what he set out to accomplish, and when the judge took the hotel owner aside following the meal and explained curtly that anyone found harboring the outlaw would find himself in deep trouble, McLeod liked the little judge even less. Dugas then told his men he would return shortly; in the meantime, the sleigh was to be readied and everyone to get aboard while he went to the post office. Warning the postmaster, Malcolm McLean, in a similar manner as he had McLeod, he then went about searching for warmer outerwear. He returned with nothing but a ladies' "cloud," or light scarf, which he wrapped about his head, not without some embarrassment.

The trip to Stornoway, ten miles distant, would have been quite uneventful had not the carryall become skittish on a particularly icy portion of road, and on swerving to the right, caught a runner and dumped the entire party in a ditch already occupied by a five-foot-deep snowdrift. Judicial bodies and the press were hurled in all directions, though essentially straight down. They took it merrily enough, however. Even Dugas saw only the humor as they brushed themselves free of the snow and uprighted the heavy wagon. They continued their journey in a far better mood.

Montreal citizens took only the weekend, after the departure of the Dugas expedition, to realize they had been duped. Hadn't the chief of police assured them back in late November or early December of 1888 that he wouldn't send his men to the Eastern Townships? Hadn't some gone anyway, ostensibly to survey the difficulties the authorities were having in capturing Morrison and then report back? What then was this "Dugas Expedition," which was headlined across every French- and English-language newspaper in town? And why was it made up exclusively of Montreal policemen? Montrealers, wanting the truth, packed the large council chambers in the city hall on Monday, April 1, to find out for themselves what was going on.

Mayor Vital Grenier greeted them with less than his usual show of vigor. Thinking the fat might be in the fire, he had placed other matters first on the agenda, hoping to discourage as many citizens as possible from staying.

The leading item concerned the start of construction on the restaurant atop Mount Royal. After much debate a bill authorizing it was passed. Then members of council tackled the thorny question of whether the Victoria Rifles (militia) should be exempt from paying taxes. Finally an exasperated alderman, William H. Cunningham, rose on a point of order, demanding council tackle the real problem at hand: the "Megantic picnic," as he called it.

Amid shouts of "yes, yes," Grenier rose to his feet, looked about him, then read aloud from a telegram he had taken from the dossier before him:

THE GOVERNMENT OF THE PROVINCE OF QUEBEC HAS INFORMA-
TION FROM JUDGE DUGAS TO THE EFFECT THAT THE MONTREAL
POLICE, WITH HIM NOW IN THE COUNTY OF COMPTON, ARE
ABSOLUTELY REQUIRED TO EFFECT THE ARREST OF MORRISON,
WHICH WE EXPECT WILL SOON BE ACCOMPLISHED. I TRUST
THAT YOUR COUNCIL WILL NOT RECALL THESE MEN BUT WILL
ALLOW THEM TO COMPLETE THE PUBLIC DUTY TO THE ACCOM-
PLISHMENT OF WHICH THEY HAVE THUS FAR SO VERY EF-
FICIENTLY CONTRIBUTED.

(SIGNED) ATTORNEY GENERAL TURCOTTE

Grenier paused, dropping the telegram dramatically to his desk as he surveyed the chamber about him. He spoke then with directness, saying how Police Chief Hughes bore the blame for sending these officers without direction from the council as a whole. It was "off-handed action," as he called it, then skillfully diverted the matter to safer ground by adding that the cost of the expedition would be covered by the city's running account with the province. As for council, he said, waving his arms about him, he was positive it would leave the police in the Eastern Townships until the business was over. Placing his hands on the desk, he waited for someone to answer. The "someone" was Alderman Stephens who rose to address the assembly.

"In the interests of justice," he said, drawing himself up to his full height, "the chief of police should be authorized to let the men stay as long as required, provided the Government reimburse their *pay* from the time they left, their travel and properly reward them for bravery."

Alderman Patrick Kennedy, sitting in the back row, saw the whitewash coming and leaped to his feet. Someone had to set this business straight, once and for all, he shouted. It was noth-

ing but a farce, a genuine farce, what with Chief Hughes sending his men "out on a picnic." "Everybody objected to the *manner* of doing this," he said, hotly. "The chairman was asked for
permission to send them out and he refused, the Chief was asked
and he at first refused, then someone suggested they be let out
on a holiday and *this* plan was adopted." Greeted with a roar of
approval from the gallery, he turned to Grenier: "I cannot see,
Mr. Mayor, that it is required to carry carbines and ammunition . . ."

"And bagpipes," snorted Alderman Cunningham.

Alexander Stevenson, yet another alderman and a Scot himself, took the floor. "And such a picnic to hunt down my fellow
countryman and why? Forsooth, because they give shelter and
food to an unfortunate man who is being hunted through the
country. The sympathies of these people cannot be controlled,
Mr. Mayor, the hospitality of the Scotsman is to be controlled as
little as the sun can be controlled in shining. If Alderman
Stevens or any other gentleman here would require it, he would
get food and shelter in any highlander's home. . . ." Stevenson's
head dropped to his chest. "There should be a limit to the time
of this expedition," he muttered.

Alderman Hormisdas Jennotte broke the somber silence. The
police should stay till maple-sugar time. No one agreed. Finally
the council settled for Saturday, April 20, with *no further exten-
sion.* Put to a vote, it passed.

A second council meeting, though more a council of war,
took place later the same day. It lacked the comforts of a warm
council chamber, held as it was in a desolate, drafty barn near
Weedon Lake several miles north of Fisher Hill. In attendance
were Donald Morrison and the original members of the Defense
Organization which included Malcolm Matheson and Hugh
Leonard. They had gathered to plan against the latest onslaught
of police whose numbers had grown to something in excess of
150 men, by a rough estimate; there were undoubtedly more.
Donald had brought them together to find out the worst and
what they thought Judge Dugas was up to.

Hugh Leonard spoke first, saying he had some firsthand experience dealing with Judge Dugas and his party. They had sud-

denly appeared in Stornoway at Leonard's Hotel (operated by his brother James) last Saturday, demanding rooms for an indefinite stay. Before the Leonard family knew what was happening, the hotel was turned into a new headquarters for the expeditionary force.

Morrison paced the dirt floor, his breath forming a cloud as he walked. But why, he wanted to know, did Dugas leave Megantic? What sort of diabolical scheme had he up his sleeve? Hugh Leonard shrugged.

Malcolm Matheson, the Megantic shop owner, settled himself down into the rotting hay, trying to block a breeze which swept in through some loose boards. He was about to fill his pipe, thought better of it, and jammed it back into his pocket. He too was puzzled when Dugas left in the Beauce and did not return. Yesterday, Sunday, the carryall was back with a man called Tremblay. He cleared out the rooms of those in the police party, at the Prince of Wales, paid the outstanding bill, then left. It was only now, said Matheson, that he knew they had gone to Stornoway.

Finlay McLeod interrupted, grumbling about the patrol which had doubled at his hotel in Spring Hill and mentioned how Dugas had warned him about aiding Morrison. McLean the postmaster roared aloud that he too had been cornered by Dugas, and in the next minute Hugh Leonard and Matheson had added their names to the "threat" roster. These simple admissions broke the tension which had been building in the barn since everyone had arrived. They knew, too, that Dugas had a good idea who was behind the Defense Organization—but *only* an idea. Donald Morrison grunted at this remark and looked purposefully at the others. There wasn't a jail in the county big *or* strong enough to hold them all, and as the chuckles died away he became serious, pleading with them to be extra cautious and not to take chances. He asked them also to spread the word to others and particularly to warn them not to tangle with Dugas, who could make it difficult for them.

Problems extended beyond the Scottish community, Hugh Leonard chimed in. Dugas was threatening the press, admittedly in a slightly different way, by telling Spanyaardt how he, the judge, had been informed "that the Scots were already incensed with correspondents and that it would be best for him not to venture too far from Leonard's Hotel." Spanyaardt had come to Hugh Leonard, asking what it meant, but Leonard had reassured the reporter that the judge was attempting to undermine everything in order to create a tide of disfavor against Morrison. Relieved, Spanyaardt promised to take no notice of Dugas. McLean, the lawyer, was the man who should remain indoors, Spanyaardt was told.

The small group huddled together in the barn far into the night, discussing, among other things, whether or not a meeting should be set with Dugas, should the occasion arise, with Morrison present. Some, like John Hamilton from Winslow, thought Morrison should never come in contact with the law, even if a truce was planned. He said he wouldn't trust any of those ruffians no matter what guarantees went with it. He had been against earlier negotiations which would have sent their friend to trial in Quebec. Looking back on it now, they all agreed that Donald had been wise not to give himself up. Matheson and Hugh Leonard felt that if Dugas called for a truce and terms could be met guaranteeing safe conduct for Donald then so be it. The meeting place would be specified by the Defense Organization and they would have enough Scots about to ensure the truce was carried out. To this some heads nodded. Angus McLeod's didn't. He said a truce would only bring members of the Defense Organization into the open. At present the police only *suspected* a number of them; they had no proof.

They argued endlessly until at last Morrison said he personally favored such a meeting with Dugas, but only under terms set down by the Defense Organization, with it stipulating time and place. If such a meeting were arranged, it would have to be done with much care and thought. Nothing could be left to chance. He didn't trust a square inch of the official ground they walked on.

False dawn had broken over Little Megantic Mountain, sending a pink glow up toward the stars, when the meeting was adjourned. It was Tuesday, April 2. Donald Morrison moved about, shaking hands with each man, asking about their families, exchanging a few personal words, and receiving in return warm assurances of support. He then went outside to thank a number of men who had braved the cold night to remain on lookout, should a patrol have come their way. By true dawn, each member of the organization was home, with no one else the wiser. As for Morrison, he had gone on to visit the Buchanans at North Hill, where he'd been invited to share a hearty breakfast.

Chief Detective Silas Carpenter got up, stretched, and walked about the tent waving his arms, hoping he hadn't lost *all* the circulation from his body. Sleeping on the ground had never thrilled him much; sleeping on frozen ground even less so. A hot breakfast at the hotel in Marsden would make him feel better; he might even talk the management into offering him a hot bath.

The canvas above Carpenter's head fluttered in a cold breeze which had broken around the corner of the stand of pines just beyond the camp ground. The detective shivered momentarily, then reached for the heavy greatcoat which had served as one of many blankets since the night of March 30. He should wear it to sleep, he thought, buttoning it high up to the collar. Once ready, he stepped over two sleeping forms lost beneath their own covers, untied the flaps, and found himself outside facing an extremely chilly Tuesday morning.

He had been on lookout until midnight, keeping an eye on Murdo Morrison's place across the way. The log cabin was a good two hundred yards away from their camp. They had erected the tent in the lee of the woods and built a fire outside which burned continuously. It had been kept alive through the night watch by a guide named Pierre Leroyer who had been hired by the expedition and attached to Carpenter's patrol Sunday. Leroyer had come into the tent at dawn, ending the surveillance on Morrison's place at dusk this evening when McMahon would take over. Meanwhile, the cold had worked into the detective's bones and the thought of eating a hot breakfast sent him off across the fields to Marsden, two miles away.

Inside the tent Pierre Leroyer, tucked in his bedroll, had heard Carpenter shuffling about, followed by silence. He waited for a good ten minutes, then pushed his blankets and bearskin away and looked around. A mound of blankets on the other side of the tent hid McMahon's sleeping form. For Leroyer, sleep came in a series of short bursts, rather than one long session.

He had slept deeply since crawling into the tent three hours before and now he was ready to move about. Within five minutes he had rebuilt the fire outside into a crackling mass of burning logs and he hunkered down on his heels close enough to feel the heat of it digging into his clothes.

Pierre Leroyer was doubtless the most able among the force for this kind of work. A local trapper and woodsman, he owed allegiance to no one. His backwoods costume of fur coat, cinched about the waist with a colorful woven belt, and Indian moccasins tethered about his feet, set him apart from others in the expedition.

He was a handsomely gaunt and wiry man, with intense dark eyes and long curly hair which flowed unevenly down over his shoulders. Added to this was a thick black mustache and long aquiline nose which made his face look narrower than it was. Most mistook Pierre Leroyer for a half-breed, an impression he didn't try to discourage, though he was pure French, having come from the valley of the Loire. He'd come to Canada seeking adventure and had headed straight into the Northwest. Befriended by Indians along the way, he learned about the nature of the land and went to work for the Hudson's Bay Company as a *coureur de bois*. As restless a man as the country around him, Leroyer finally came back to Quebec and the Eastern Townships, where he was hired as guide, trapper, and general man-about-the-woods for the predominantly American Megantic Fish and Game Club in nearby Three Lakes.

He came strongly recommended by Police Chief Hughes who had met the guide on several occasions in Montreal. Dugas needed a good man who was as much at home in the Eastern Townships as Morrison. The judge offered Leroyer a salary far exceeding the guide's expectations. In accepting the offer his only worry was finding someone to care for his dependents back in his cabin in Three Lakes: four bears, two deer, a porcupine, two agile monkeys, and a moose. Dugas promised they would be looked after—in one way or another.

The Frenchman actually joined the expeditionary force in Montreal, where he was hired, and was the center of interest during the trip to the Eastern Townships. Rumors made the rounds that he was a fearless half-breed guide who was expected to track the outlaw right into his lair. But sitting here by the fire, Pierre Leroyer wondered where all his importance had gone. Tracking didn't mean sitting on one's butt as he had done for the past twenty-four hours. And what irked him more was this: while he remained here keeping an eye on the log house across the way, the police and others were tripping over one another in search of the $2,000 reward money (rumors put it as high as $3,000) and Morrison, possibly in that order. It was the reward more than his salary and paid expenses which had brought about Leroyer's decision to join the expedition; it annoyed him to be placed here in virtual limbo.

While Leroyer sat brooding over his lot in the Marsden camp, ten miles away, near North Hill, young Willy McAulay was brooding about school. He was supposed to be there now, but instead he'd been following a snowshoe rabbit's track until he had lost all sense of time. Finally he had turned back and was making his way slowly toward his destination, trying to dream up a better excuse than usual why he was late, when he spied "bluecoats" coming up the road from Gould. For a moment he stood stock still, wondering why it made him upset. Patrols hadn't been around here all week, so why all the fuss?

Willy's brain raced backwards, trying to pick up odd bits of conversation he'd heard around the breakfast table that morning. Bluecoats! Hadn't his father mentioned something about Donald Morrison being over at the John Buchanan's? Right here in North Hill?

Whirling around once more, Willy took off across the field, fighting his way over the receding snowdrifts, floundering and falling and picking himself up again. The police were still far enough back on that road up from Gould, not the main road, but a secondary one used more in the winter because it was protected better from the surrounding hills.

At last he reached home, and stumbled straight toward the barn. Within minutes he had the harness on the team of horses and was pulling them back into position on either side of the oak tongue attached to the flatbed sleigh. His mother, attracted by the sudden noise outside, reached the kitchen window just in time to see her son and sleigh go plunging by toward the road, leaving her to wonder what his excuse would be *this* time for not being in school.

It was a wild-eyed Willy McAulay who dragged the team to a savage stop outside the Buchanan's place. Moments later Donald Morrison himself climbed aboard and directed Willy to swing the horses 'round and head for the road. Willy grinned and slapped the leather reins along the broad backs of the team. They had no sooner reached the road when through a clearing both Willy and Donald could see far across the fields the police sleigh plodding toward the intersection which would bring them down in their direction.

Willy couldn't believe his ears when Morrison told him to turn left, setting the horses in the direction of the approaching police sleigh. Morrison grinned. If they turned *right*, into North Hill, they would be trapped by a dead end. No, with any luck he and Willy and the team of horses might be able to make it by the intersecting road before the police got there.

The Buchanans', and North Hill beyond it, fell away as the flatbed sleigh moved ponderously along the road. The vehicle had no seats. Both Willy and Morrison leaned against shoulder-high racks in the front, their knees up tight against the lowest crossbar. Five minutes later they were within a hundred yards of the intersection. A casual glance off to the right told Donald that the sleigh full of policemen, on this road, wasn't much further from the intersection either. It was Donald's hope to be *through* the intersection and continuing eastward before the other sleigh had arrived there. His chances didn't look promising.

Fifty yards to go. Donald could see out of the corner of his eye the sun glistening off the rifle barrels and brass buttons of the dark coats. He felt Willy shift uneasily beside him and prayed that the lad's nerve wouldn't snap, that he wouldn't panic and whip the horses into a gallop. At this range those rifles would blast them both clear off the sleigh.

Twenty-five yards. Morrison could feel his heart pounding wildly in his chest. Slowly he slipped a mitted hand inside his coat and felt the bony hardness of the Colt's butt. For once he wished he hadn't gotten the habit of leaving the second revolver hidden for safekeeping in the McIver's barn in Spring Hill.

Almost at once he withdrew the hand and laughing aloud

clapped the startled Will McAulay merrily across the shoulders. Willy took up the lead and began laughing too. At the same time he slapped the reins and made clicking noises with his mouth, urging the horses on a little faster.

Aboard the Beauce carryall, High Constable Adolphe Bissonette squirmed uncomfortably in his seat next the driver, wondering what had ever possessed him to accept Dugas' offer of coming to this part of the province—then to be thrust outside in such weather to search for a bloody phantom. Breakfast was served this Tuesday morning in Stornoway while it was still dark outside. Dugas had suggested a patrol should be sent out toward Gould, then up to North Hill, with Bissonette in charge. The high constable needed to familiarize himself with the countryside and this would be a fine opportunity to do so. Without waiting for Bissonette to reply, Dugas turned to Captain Giroux, asking him to muster a patrol. The carryall was at their disposal.

Dawn had hardly dinted the darkness when the captain reported to Bissonette that the Beauce was ready. With them would be Sherbrooke police Constables, Demers, Logan, "Tall" McEwan (a "Short" McEwan was also attached to the expedition), and several volunteers from the Sherbrooke militia.

On reaching Gould some time after eight o'clock, Bissonette called for a rest near the old grist mill found in a gully west of town. Then they moved on toward North Hill, with the intention of swinging to East Dudswell, then back to Gould and finally Stornoway before nightfall. It was nine-thirty when the sleigh cleared a rise and off to his left Bissonette saw a small cluster of buildings across the fields. North Hill. Already they were behind schedule and at this speed they weren't likely to reach East Dudswell, let alone get back to Gould by nightfall. Annoyed and cold, the high constable told the driver to get more speed out of the horses.

The pace quickened and, satisfied, Bissonette pulled the robes tight around him as he let his mind drift away from the realities of this cold and inordinately miserable outing. He had hoped to spend Sunday indoors, catching up on his reports and browsing through several handfuls of letters taken from a trunk he'd found the other day in the elder Morrison's log house

near Marsden. He had confiscated letters addressed to the outlaw from an Augusta McIver and some from William Matheson
of Winslow, among others. These might contain hints of Morrison's whereabouts or at least some routine . . .

A nudge tore Bissonette from his reverie as Giroux, seated
beside him, pointed to a farm sleigh moving toward the intersection ahead and to their immediate left. Two men were leaning
against the rack of the sleigh laughing and jostling one another,
apparently oblivious of the approaching police. The man closest
to them, the high constable noticed, appeared to be holding his
sides with hilarity of the moment. Well, they wouldn't be so
happy in a very few minutes, he thought to himself. He would
have them stopped at the crossroads for a brief interrogation.
In the meantime he would just sit back and relax, close his eyes
and think of places he'd rather be.

It was short-lived. Captain Giroux nudged him again. Bissonette opened his eyes. The other sleigh must have speeded up
for it was already at the crossroads. Angry with himself, the high
constable told the driver to go faster, then looked behind to see
his men had their rifles at the ready. The sleigh jerked and
bumped about as the horses broke into a trot. Bissonette, helped
by Giroux, got shakily to his feet, waving his arms and yelling
for the other sleigh to halt, but his words were lost unfortunately
to the wind and all he received in return were waves and
delighted muffled shouts from the pair aboard the other sleigh
who then turned ahead and didn't look back.

Bissonette had the Beauce halted at the crossroads. They
could easily overtake the flatbed sleigh, the driver and Giroux
were telling him together. If he'd just sit down . . . !

Bissonette eased himself back onto the seat, drawing the
blankets tight around him. Angry at himself for missing the opportunity to detain his first set of "locals," he decided against
pursuit. Head left for North Hill, he ordered, otherwise they
wouldn't make it back to Gould for supper. And after a day in
this sleigh, a good hot meal would be one small comfort for such
a miserable time.

Tuesday, April 2 hadn't been all that kind to Judge Aimée
Dugas in Stornoway either. He had yet to hear from the first

patrol he'd sent out at midnight, and deciding he would wait
no longer, he was stretching himself out for an afternoon nap
when the sound of clinking harness brought him off the bed
and over to the window. As he pulled back the curtain he saw
Peter Spanyaardt climbing into a sleigh. Dugas cursed. Where
the hell was *he* going? And how the devil did Spanyaardt
always manage transportation when the police couldn't put their
hands on a sleigh for love nor money? Still mumbling to himself, Dugas shifted his eyes to the man holding the reins. He'd
seen him earlier and asked who he was. The blacksmith, he was
told, William Matheson from nearby Winslow. Well, he certainly was big enough. And *another* Matheson? He'd never
seen anything like it. If a man wasn't a Matheson or a Mac-
Donald, he was a McRitchie, McLeod, or some such name.
How the dickens did they tell each other apart? Already he'd
heard of five John MacDonalds and how many McIvers? He
had lost track.

On impulse Dugas shot across the room, yanked the door
open wide, and bellowed down the hall for Bissonette, then realized he was on patrol. He shouted for Giroux next, only to
remember he too was gone. Slamming the door he plodded bare-
footed back to the window in time to see the small sleigh turning
south at the corner, heading toward Spring Hill. That damned
reporter, he swore to himself, as he trundled back to bed. His
men had been given strict orders to give no information to the
press (other reporters were constantly drifting in and out of the
Eastern Townships, covering the Morrison story), and still
Spanyaardt popped up with news reports from all over the area.
Well, let something big happen, and Spanyaardt would be the
last one to hear about it. He would guarantee it, Dugas thought.

By late afternoon Spanyaardt and William Matheson had arrived at McLeod's Hotel on the Drumavack Road in Spring Hill
where they warmed themselves by the stove after a chilling ride
down from Stornoway. Feeling better, Spanyaardt had left the
blacksmith ten minutes later and sat down to work on his story
when the front door yawned open and a handful of frozen
policemen tumbled in, heading directly for the stove. Spanyaardt
glanced up, then returned to his work. When he looked up a second time a police sergeant stood over him.

The reporter introduced himself and learned the sergeant's name was Leggatt. He was a rangy sort of man who obviously enjoyed being in command of this small detachment. When asked what he had been up to, Leggatt hedged, saying only he and his men had been on a twelve-mile patrol.

Was it true, Spanyaardt asked, that Morrison had some new kind of magazine-loading rifle? Leggatt shrugged his shoulders; he'd never tell if he *did* know. He wasn't about to tell this reporter anything, as the judge had ordered. Spanyaardt smiled and joined William Matheson by the stove. He told his companion in whispered tones that he would return shortly; he wanted to make some inquiries around town. Matheson nodded and watched the reporter step around the police and head for the door.

He was back within twenty minutes. He settled himself in a large chair and for the next five minutes wrote without removing either coat or hat. Leggatt smiled to himself, wondering what the reporter would say since he was without any information.

But Peter Spanyaardt hid his delight. He'd learned what he wanted and the story would make tomorrow's headline.

> SPRING HILL, Que., April 2—There was another midnight expedition Monday night, but still Morrison is at large. It has become absolutely impossible to obtain any official news, but though received from other sources, my information will be found as correct as that which could be obtained from Judge Dugas directly. The constables have been instructed not to tell me anything, and information is systematically denied on the ground that it will hurt the result of the expedition.

Spanyaardt also told of Saturday's bitterly cold sleigh ride from Megantic, the luncheon in Spring Hill, and the spill beyond. He gave his impressions of the people and Dugas' statement that the press wasn't welcomed by the community. He told of a midnight patrol, a request for reinforcements, and saved

Leggatt for last. The man's obvious smugness had annoyed him and he added two lines which he hoped would indicate to some that the sergeant might be enjoying himself far more than he should down here in the Eastern Townships. At least under the circumstances.

> . . . and Sergeant Leggatt and his men seem to be perfectly at home at McLeod's Hotel. . . .

Judge Aimée Dugas was not impressed with the story when it appeared in Wednesday's *Star*. He liked it less that the police weren't tackling the situation with as much effort as were he and his immediate staff. The Scots community too had proved to be a great hindrance over the past few days and *that* was something Dugas would not tolerate.

10

"TO AID AND ABET"

APRIL 1889

J. Sidney Broderick couldn't sleep. His body itched and his mind feverishly reviewed legal cases past and present. Finally he threw aside the covers and wandered barefoot down to the kitchen. If he couldn't sleep, he'd eat. His creation of the perfect sandwich was well underway when he imagined hearing a knock at the front door. It couldn't be the door at this hour. It was just after 5 A.M. The knock came again. Clutching his robe he padded out into the vestibule and opened the door. From the shadows of darkness came an outstretched hand bearing a telegram marked "URGENT." He accepted the envelope and the hand slipped back into the darkness.

Sidney Broderick took both sandwich and telegram back to the kitchen, lit a second lamp, took a bite from the sandwich, and placed it carefully down on the table. Whoever sent the telegram must have some influence somewhere, he thought, having it delivered in Sherbrooke at this hour of the morning. He unfolded it and the name "SPANYAARDT" caught his attention, then the place of origin, SPRING HILL, and the date, APRIL 4, 1889.

All at once he was fully awake. His eyes quickly scanned the message, but saw no mention of Morrison. He went back to the beginning. Arrests had begun among members of the Scottish community. Spanyaardt listed three men, none of whom Broderick knew. They were charged with "aiding and abetting" a man accused of murder. Spanyaardt asked the lawyer to help them. They had been taken into custody at 3 A.M. and were now heading by train for Sherbrooke, and jail, via Scotstown.

The lawyer read the message several times, then sat down slowly at the kitchen table. He'd been following the Morrison business avidly through Peter Spanyaardt's newspaper reports and, knowing Dugas professionally, he often wondered when the judge would attack and how. This telegram answered both questions. Dugas would send every last Scotsman in the Eastern Townships to jail if need be, until he accomplished his assignment. These three, thought Broderick, picking up his sandwich in both hands, would be only the first of many.

Sleep was also a scarce commodity for the Finlay McLeods of Spring Hill in the early hours of Thursday morning, April 4. At 2 A.M. Finlay was prowling aimlessly about the hotel lobby wondering why things had gone wrong—again. He and Mrs. McLeod had been at each other's throats for the past couple of weeks over his strong defense of Donald Morrison, a view she found offensive. Besides, she hadn't been well lately and arguing only made him feel as if he was taking advantage of her poor health. On the other hand, he knew it was a hopeless stalemate because she was the niece of Major Malcolm McAulay and he, Finlay, wasn't about to relinquish his own principles for the sake of family unity.

Having the police encamped on his doorstep hadn't helped the situation. It was another of those late-night expeditions leaving the hotel at midnight which precipitated the latest argument. With preparations for the patrol going on below, Mrs. McLeod had casually remarked how for everyone's sake, she hoped Morrison would be caught "this time." Finlay, taking exception, leaped from the bed and stormed about the room telling her how ruthless she was in her talk about an innocent man and what he thought of her uncle and family. She countered with a few deft observations of her own, and only his quitting the room brought the battle to an end, at least for the moment.

By the time he reached the lobby a wave of guilt swept over him. He knew such conflict did neither of them any good. Why couldn't he learn to ignore her taunts instead of jumping in with both feet and giving her the satisfaction of having triggered the desired reaction. No, he mustn't take it so seriously after this.

Feeling better, he decided to give her time to settle down before going back upstairs. In the meantime, the kitchen beckoned with promises of delightful snacks. The kitchen door squeaked as he entered.

It was after 2:30 when he stepped back into the lobby, the earlier confrontation now a half-forgotten family spat. He looked around the now-quiet room lit by the dull glow of the oil lamps hinged to the walls, then started for the stairway. Barely had he reached the first step when the door opened and in walked Sergeant Leggatt and his men. McLeod smiled and was about to continue upstairs when the reflection in the sergeant's face made him stop. He looked back. Leggatt was walking awkwardly across the lobby floor as though nursing a kicked shin. Leggatt stopped, his eyes failing to hold to the innkeeper's as he muttered something about arrest on charges of aiding a fugitive. McLeod almost laughed. "*Who* was arrested?" he asked, not having caught the name. Leggatt looked at him blankly. "*You,* sir," the sergeant repeated.

Less than twenty minutes later Spring Hill postmaster Malcolm McLean was rousted from a deep sleep and prodded into his clothes. His protests were to no avail. Shortly after three o'clock he stood in the lobby of McLeod's Hotel listening to his friend Finlay explode in all directions.

McLeod was pointing to the couch where his wife sat crumpled in tears. McLeod shouted over and over that she was ill and needed someone to look after her. He couldn't *leave* on such short notice. Maybe by morning. . . .

But Leggatt had his orders. They would have to leave then. He was sorry but . . . McLeod ignored him. He walked to his wife and bent down, bringing his hand gently up under her chin. She looked at him, her face awash with tears. Leaning forward he kissed her wet cheek.

Only when the buffalo robes were wrapped tightly around them a few minutes later did Finlay look at Malcolm McLean with a smile hidden in the corners of his mouth. They had done the right thing, he said over and over, as they headed for the railway station, no matter how it would turn out. He knew also that the neighbors, already in the hotel, would look after his sick wife.

Spanyaardt and Allardice were also busy that Thursday. The latter had set off for Sherbrooke the moment Peter Spanyaardt had reached him at his hotel in Marsden, around five in the morning. His story of what had occurred during the night made the early edition of the Montreal *Star*.

PRISONERS AT SHERBROOKE

SHERBROOKE, Que., April 4—Constables Albert McKeown, of the Montreal police detachment and G. W. Beard of the Megantic Force, arrived here this morning with John Hamilton, millwright, Finlay McLeod, hotel keeper, and Malcolm McLean, postmaster, all three arrested for harboring Donald Morrison and, it is understood, committed for further examination before a magistrate here, having undergone a preliminary examination before Judge Dugas. An application for bail made to the latter by the prisoners was refused. The evidence adduced against Malcolm McLean was especially strong. J. Sidney Broderick, advocate of this city, had been retained to defend them.

Four men met in the back of Malcolm Matheson's store in Megantic that Thursday night: the storekeeper, Murdo Beaton, Hugh Leonard, and Donald Morrison. Megantic had become one of the safer spots for Morrison these days, though he still moved in and out of the village like a shadow. He had arrived shortly after dark. Matheson had closed the door behind him, locked it, and led Morrison into his office. The others were already there. They nodded, not knowing quite what to say.

Morrison was clearly upset. Three arrested and more to come, he said. Dugas was shrewd, knowing where it would hurt the most. Matheson agreed, but wanted Morrison to know the Defense Organization had been in touch with Sidney Broderick through Spanyaardt, and he'd be looking after Finlay McLeod, Malcolm McLean, and John Hamilton. Hugh Leonard, sitting on the edge of Matheson's roll-top desk, said he would be getting in touch with his younger brother, John, the lawyer. Bail money was already being gathered . . . Morrison shook his head and laughed. Dugas hadn't gone to the trouble of slapping them in jail to have them released on *bail*, he said. The judge would hold onto them by every means at his disposal. Murdo Beaton, standing on guard by the shaded window, muttered about the Defense Organization's losing three of its key men. But damn it, he said, it wasn't going to be so easy for the police. He'd been speaking to *many* Scots who were willing to go to jail no matter what. Dugas would soon find his hands full and they'd raise such a fuss . . . !

Morrison turned to Malcolm Matheson. He didn't like these arrests, aimed surely at discouraging the Scots community from supporting him. But did it go deeper than this?

Matheson thought for a moment, then looked at Hugh Leonard who nodded back. Matheson then addressed himself to Morrison. He had heard that the judge was angling for a meeting between himself and Morrison. The arrests were to spur on such a meeting, knowing Morrison would want to plead for his friends' release. But the second reason for the arrests was to give Dugas some leverage in dealing with Morrison. In other words "collateral," said Matheson, with a grim smile. The arrests wouldn't stop there. Dugas was putting on the pressure. Now the question was, when Dugas asked for a meeting, was Donald willing to accept it? Morrison nodded. Leonard was pleased. Murdo Beaton stood alone in opposition. Morrison however wanted one thing clear. His terms stood fast: either the family farm was returned to him or Major McAulay paid him back the $900. Donald would then "disappear" and never be a bother to anyone again. And he wouldn't give himself up to Dugas either.

The Defense Organization didn't have long to wait. On Friday, April 5, Malcolm Matheson looked up from his counter to find Judge Dugas entering the store. Without a word Matheson waved him into his small office. He didn't offer him a chair. Dugas came immediately to the point: he was willing for a truce so he and Morrison could talk. Matheson agreed, but on Morrison's terms. Dugas' eyes narrowed. Matheson's could be the next name on the arrest list, he countered, but the threat brought only a smile from the storekeeper.

Dugas grudgingly admired Matheson's quiet persistence. He knew the man would go to jail without a murmur. In fact, the whole damn Scots community could be jailed en masse, and the reaction would be the same. Already the judge had learned that families of the jailed men were being looked after by neighbors who had taken over the husbands' chores. Angered, he had drawn up another forty-five warrants which were ready to be served at a moment's notice. Did Matheson know he had personally ordered the arrest of William Matheson, the Winslow blacksmith, and John McLeod of Dell? Malcolm Matheson didn't answer.

During the next few days Morrison managed a brief stop at his parents' home near Marsden. Forewarned, Sophia dimmed the lamps early. Donald stayed but a short time. Sophia hugged him close, then watched her son walk over to his father. They murmured to one another, then Donald spent the remaining moments with his mother. They talked about the family and a possible truce. Before he left he told her he would spend a few days with Colin Campbell who was pioneering a new site far above Red Mountain. It would be safe there. Then he was gone.

Meanwhile Dugas and Co. had moved its headquarters to Gould in an effort to keep the Scots guessing. Another twenty-five provincial police had arrived from Quebec, along with several militia volunteers who came down for the sport—and the reward. Several days earlier the Quebec government had hired some detectives from Pinkerton's, the private American agency, and these, numbering about a dozen, were presently en route to the Eastern Townships. Their arrival would put the total force under Dugas' command at more than two hundred men.

Along with them, arrests escalated: John Hammond of Lingwick (the fourth original member of the Defense Organization),

Murdo MacArthur of Winslow, and Peter Matheson of Megantic. Sherbrooke jail was taking on the appearance of a meeting of the clans.

It was over Sunday breakfast in McCoy's Hotel in Gould that Peter Spanyaardt heard about Angus McLeod's arrest the previous afternoon, the sixth of April. Serious though it was, his escapade that ended in his arrest was the talk of Gould this morning and told with admiration. The crowded hotel dining room was humming with the story.

Angus McLeod, a crafty little Scot from North Hill, known for his boundless energy, was a man truly committed to helping Donald Morrison's cause no matter where or when. On Saturday it had been his turn.

It was a fairly mild day and enough snow had melted to allow him to replace his sleigh with a small wagon. He could have used either. Having some errands to run to Bury, he hitched up his team of horses, known for their speed and spirit, and set off hoping they might settle down by the time they reached the Gould–Bury road. On turning west toward Bury they were still full of vinegar, so he let them have a gallop to wear off some of their enthusiasm.

They hadn't gone a mile when McLeod noticed someone snowshoeing across the fields and he waved, realizing it was Donald Morrison. He reined in his team, which took some doing, and the two men talked for a while. McLeod offered him a lift, but Morrison said he was enjoying the walk. Angus McLeod went on and hadn't gone two miles when he passed a wagon crammed with bluecoats. The police watched him go by, turn, and pull abreast, shouting that he'd seen Morrison a little way down the road and if they hurried, they might catch him.

What happened next was difficult to believe. Yelling that they could catch Morrison *if* they beat *him* to the outlaw, the old Scot flipped the reins and his team broke away as though fired from a cannon. McLeod did reach Morrison first and was hauling him aboard when the second wagon came flying over the rise, less than two hundred yards away. McLeod, they said, took the road left to North Hill on two wheels and disappeared into the rolling hills. When the police finally cornered McLeod, sit-

ting calm as you please by the roadside on the outskirts of North
Hill, he was smoking his pipe and talking to his horses. Asked
about the outlaw, Angus McLeod had screwed up his face and
asked, "Who?" insisting he didn't know any outlaw. By early
Sunday morning he had joined his friends for breakfast—in the
Sherbrooke jail.

The story brought great chuckles from the reporter. A moment of levity never hurt anyone, he insisted, as he wiped the
last traces of egg from his mouth. Someone else suggested the
police might consider arresting the entire Canadian Pacific Railway system, because it was well known that Morrison often
evaded his captors by riding on freight cars or, on occasion, even
in passenger compartments. The reporter's second burst of laughter earned him scowls from the police at nearby tables, so he politely excused himself and went outside for some fresh air.
Thinking it might be wise to remove himself from Gould for the
day, he went down to the local livery stable to rent a horse and
set out for Marsden.

He found Allardice in good shape, though exhausted from accompanying a night patrol out of Scotstown, a request made by
the Montreal *Star* editor for a personal story. They talked until
Allardice was on the verge of falling asleep. Spanyaardt finally
wished him good-night and left. By midafternoon he arrived at
Leonard's Hotel in Stornoway.

To his surprise he found Chief Detective Silas Carpenter,
Constable James McMahon, and the guide Pierre Leroyer lounging about the veranda drinking. They insisted Spanyaardt join
them and when he asked casually what they had been up to,
Carpenter laughed, saying they had all been on a "special mission" and had taken the remainder of the day off. "Unofficially,"
Carpenter added, winking. During the conversation the reporter
wondered aloud if anyone else was staying at the hotel and was
told that Sub-Chief Lancy was now in charge of the Stornoway
detachment and that High Constable Hiram Moe, both from
Sherbrooke, had spent the night. A moment later Moe and Lancy
joined them, and after introductions, the high constable leaned
over to Spanyaardt, asking him if he'd heard the latest story
making the rounds? At least in police circles? Peter smiled, no,

he hadn't. Moe took a deep breath and was about to launch into a recitation when Sub-Chief Lancy interrupted. No one in the expeditionary force was permitted to say anything to the press, he said indignantly. Without turning, Hiram Moe remarked he *wasn't* part of the expeditionary force (which brought a round of applause from the others) and began. It concerned one of Donald Morrison's relatives, a farmer who lived close to the parent's home in Marsden, he said with a chuckle. At the moment the relative was on a retainer from the police and was expected to pass on any pertinent information about Morrison—who was aiding him, his whereabouts, anything. For this he was paid $700 cash. Not wanting his wife to know, the farmer hid the cash safely away in the hay in a corner of his barn. Several days later he returned to find the hay missing and rushed to his wife who told him she had fed it to the cow. With cries of despair, the farmer rushed back to the stable. Patiently he sat behind the cow for the next forty-eight hours waiting for the animal to pass the money. By this time Moe had his audience in fits of laughter— even Lancy had trouble keeping a sober face. Spanyaardt, finally wiping away the tears, asked if anything had come out of the farmer's vigil, which set them all off once more.

The jovial atmosphere continued throughout the evening supper at Leonard's, with everyone adding his own humorous anecdote. Carpenter described how a few nights back he was searching for Morrison and had taken a wrong turn to find himself up to his neck in Otter Lake's mud and silt. McMahon wondered if it were true that Sergeant Clarke, now stationed at Gould, was still insisting on waking up the town early to the tunes of his bagpipes. Spanyaardt could attest to it, he said, being one of the many victims of the dreadful noise.

With the meal finished, Carpenter suggested they might ride to Ayres' sugarbush for a snack of maple syrup. The response was unanimous. The strain on each man for the past weeks warranted a little relaxation.

"Yankee" Ayres greeted them soberly at the small cabin back in the woods south of Spring Hill. A large cast-iron pot of boiling maple syrup sent clouds of aromatic steam high into the surrounding trees and it wasn't long before the syrup was poured on the snow and the men, armed with wood spoons, used them to roll the sticky mess around in the melting ice, then eat the iced maple syrup.

Peter Spanyaardt took his leave long before the party broke up. Though these men had done their best not to let any pertinent information leak out during the evening, Spanyaardt had learned that a truce was in the planning stages between Judge Dugas and Donald Morrison, though negotiations were thought to be going poorly.

It was close to 11:00 P.M., April 7, when Peter Spanyaardt returned to Gould. He found it difficult to believe that this was the same quiet village he had left this morning. Walking up from the livery stable he watched three large carryalls rumble by and he counted more than twenty-four policemen, eleven "volunteers" from the 1st Company of the 9th Quebec Regiment, plus a handful of bounty hunters. Among these recruits, he learned later, were prison guards who had shown interest in capturing the outlaw. Roughly, then, the reporter figured the expeditionary force must now number at least three hundred men.

More than half of these were presently being billeted in Gould, and Spanyaardt could hardly make his way up the narrow main street. He bumped shoulders and tried vainly to keep himself out of the path of prancing horses, wagons, and sleighs.

The reporter searched in vain for either Dugas or Bissonette. Finally he learned they were closeted in the judge's room in McCoy's Hotel officially signing twenty-two more warrants against those known to be harboring the outlaw. Dugas, it seemed, had publically announced that afternoon that should Morrison wound or kill any of his men, "those who willingly had given him food, shelter, arms, or ammunition would be arrested and held as accessories to attempted murder—or accessories to *murder.*"

McCoy's was jammed from wall to wall with soldiers and police, a strange assortment of gray-bearded veterans and smooth-faced rookies. The place was bedlam: laughs and yells, orders of command intermixed with orders for drinks, waving arms, and stepped-on toes and friendly elbows in the stomach or chest. These men sported every variety of headgear—regulation military issue, stiff-brimmed prison-guard hats, forage caps and fur caps and homemade woolen toques knit hurriedly by dutiful wives.

The strange assortment of headgear was matched only by the wide variety of weapons. The military men carried the new compact Snider center-fire rifle, while others preferred the shorter Remington carbines or Marlin top-ejection repeating rifles. The *kind* of rifle didn't matter, one grinning bounty hunter told Spanyaardt, just as long as it shot straight. The police themselves moved about the streets of Gould like walking arsenals, bedecked in cartridge belts, rifles, and sidearms—cheap .38-caliber Belgian "bulldog" revolvers, small pocket cannons with interchangeable barrels, or the popular long-snouted Colt Frontier Scouts.

Adventurers from beyond the Eastern Townships crawled out of everywhere, appetites whetted with distorted visions of tracking human game. They came with suitcases and trunks; they plagued authorities for photographs or a description of the wanted outlaw, so they wouldn't shoot the wrong man. Lodgings were booked to capacity, with hardly space enough to spread a blanket in the entire village. One of Bissonette's aides, the reporter learned, had taken over an entire house and crammed it full of personnel. "Every inch of available floor is used for sleeping purposes," one report to the *Star* said, "and it was only after grandly discussing the pros and cons that it was finally decided not to use the piano [for sleeping] for fear the happy possessor might roll on the keys and disturb the rest."

Stranded in the middle of this chaos and knowing he wouldn't have a hope of confirming the situation with either Dugas or Bissonette, Peter Spanyaardt pushed his way up the crowded stairway of McCoy's Hotel, intent on making sure his room hadn't been commandeered by one authority or another. He heard from the clerk downstairs that half a dozen men was the going number per room.

Judge Dugas had spent a goodly portion of his Sunday behind the bolted door of his tiny hotel room planning for the additional influx of personnel, making travel arrangements, and deciding with Bissonette which warrants should be authorized for the next batch of arrests. They also established additional "field commanders," including Captains Giroux and Haigham,

Lieutenant Blouin, and Constable Logan. These men were duly assembled in the small room, with Dugas peering around to see who was missing. At once he asked for the Marsden detail, Carpenter, McMahon, and Leroyer. Bissonette reminded Dugas that he had sent them on a night patrol east of Winslow and they had yet to report back to Marsden. Dugas shook his head. It mattered little, he said, turning his attention to the rest of the men. He told them to expect a truce to be made with Morrison and a subsequent meeting to take place between himself and the outlaw. Word as to whether the man would accept such a deal would be here by midnight, in less than an hour. Expect, too, he said slowly, that the meeting will produce *no change at all*. It wasn't even worth it, he muttered, as he walked to the window and looked at the crowded street below. Hearing whispers behind him, he interrupted saying, the meeting was being arranged primarily for "higher authorities," to "give them something to chew on."

Dugas then retraced his steps back to the bed and picked up a handful of warrants. He and Bissonette had compiled a dossier of names including all those who were known to have aided Donald Morrison in even the remotest way. These warrants were now "active." If and when the meeting with the outlaw proved inconclusive, every man jack on the expeditionary force would be part of an intensive search which would blanket the area like a snowstorm. And each of these warrants, with more to come, he said, shaking them in his hands, would send more men or women to jail than anyone could imagine—for an indefinite stay.

Bissonette now took over. The "trap," roughly the area which was involved in the search, would hereafter be divided into five regions, each headed by a commander. Carpenter would remain in Marsden with McMahon and Leroyer, Lancy in Stornoway, Leggatt in Spring Hill. The remainder would take up positions at Red Mountain and Weedon. Headquarters, under the over-all command of Dugas, would remain here in Gould, an earlier plan to move to Scotstown being scrapped. As for himself, Bissonette, he would be in charge of a roving patrol, as before. This plan would take effect the moment negotiations broke down with Donald Morrison and his Defense Organization. That is, he said, muffling a cough, with what was left of the Morrison Defense Organization.

Midnight. Judge Dugas closed the door on the last of his guests and yawned his way to the closet. He changed into his night attire and climbed into bed. His head hadn't so much as reached the pillow when he heard a sharp rapping on his door. Stifling a bellow, he got out of bed, crossed the room and opened the door to find Constable Edward Summerville, of the Quebec provincial police, standing discreetly back in the middle of the hall. There was a man in the lobby with an important message, Summerville said, his voice pitched low. His name, asked Dugas. Malcolm Matheson was the reply. The judge's chin went up and down in a quick series of nods. He'd be right down, he said, closing the door. As he got dressed, he promised himself that *should* the meeting with Morrison fail, he could also seek authorization from Quebec to establish martial law in the area. By God, he really would.

Donald Morrison's brief stay at the isolated bush camp of Colin Campbell, many miles north of Red Mountain, did him more good than he would readily admit. He had arrived at the camp Saturday afternoon, April 6, after persuading Angus McLeod to drop him south of Red Mountain and get out of the area before the police tracked down him and his wagon. He last saw the small farmer disappearing over the crest of a hill, whooping and hollering as though drawing the police off in an other direction.

His "holiday" with Campbell lasted three days. Free from the fear of capture, Donald set about felling and clearing trees with the energy of three men. Campbell, a compact, appealing Scot, insisted he rest, but from sunrise to sunset there was no stopping Morrison. He found the work invigorating and appreciated Campbell for not feeling the need to make polite conversation. Silence, at times, suited him better.

By Tuesday afternoon, April 9, clean-shaven and feeling better than he had for some time, Morrison thanked his friend and set out through the bush, intent on keeping a good distance between himself and Gould by working his way east of Magill Lake and down toward Dell.

It had been almost eleven months since he was forced to shoot Warren in Megantic. He'd been on the run for more than a year. The strain now showed in the lines etched around his mouth and eyes. Constant harassment had kept him on the move and patience had become a vital part of his life—the interminable waiting, motionless, as police scoured the land around him. He had learned much about himself: his strength of will to keep going, his ability to trust in others. At first he had relied heavily on the Defense Organization to keep him informed about the activity of the police. Then the Scots community had come to his rescue, and he'd never gone anywhere without shelter and food waiting.

As time passed he had discovered something else. Being the *hunted*, he had always to be one step ahead. In the beginning it had been easy. These days it was difficult. The hunters were everywhere. They moved incessantly, each within his allotted area. Now, too, the Scots community was under siege. Many of his supporters had been rousted out of their beds and taken off to jail. Morrison wondered, as he warily skirted Magill Lake, how he could ever repay these people who had suffered so much for him and for what they believed in.

One dear old friend who lived nearby could not be bypassed. Even if the police were encircling her homestead, Morrison would not be prevented from paying this friend a visit. Mrs. Campbell was a plucky little creature whose warmth and affection bubbled up in her like an artesian well. He approached the log cabin from her barn, moving cautiously, then, spotting no danger, knocked on her door. He heard the rustling of stiff cloth, the door latch move upward, and, as the door opened, a shriek of delight. Unlike most of her kin, outward display of emotion didn't embarrass her, and she wrapped her arms about Donald and squeezed as though he were the only man in her life. They laughed together and drank tea.

The water was boiling for a second pot when a noise outside brought them both up short. At once Mrs. Campbell sprang across the room to peer out the window. When she looked back she announced that the police had arrived. Just as calmly she told him to get under the couch; she would handle it. Before going to the door, she took one of the cups from the table, wiped it clean with her "cloud" and put it in the cupboard. Donald, in the meantime, struggled to hide his person under the low lounge at the back of the room. When he thought he'd succeeded, he lay motionless, listening to the door opening and Mrs. Campbell's greeting, in English, treating the visitors though they were all old friends.

The policemen entered but politely refused the tea. They looked about while she talked about the weather and the crops. But when she looked toward the lounge she saw Donald Morrison's boots protruding from beneath. Her heart fluttered, but her conversation missed not a beat. The police, four or five, were spreading out. One had changed course and was heading back toward Morrison's hiding place.

The lady was one step ahead of him. Cutting him off as clean as you please, she stopped by the couch and neatly dropped the hem of her dress over the protruding boots. Then she smiled and sat down, saying to him, *"Tarruing a steach do chassan."* He stopped abruptly and stared at her. She repeated it and smiled disarmingly at the others. Finally, one of them told her they didn't know Gaelic and excused themselves. As they headed for the door, she breathed a sigh of relief. Had they spoken Gaelic they would have known she was telling someone to pull in his feet.

Donald Morrison was nowhere to be found, a grim Malcolm Matheson told Judge Aimée Dugas at noon Tuesday. They had searched everywhere since just past midnight Sunday when he and the judge had agreed on the truce and subsequent meeting. But Morrison had disappeared. Would it not be possible to extend the deadline for Morrison's answer from Tuesday midnight until Wednesday noon? Dugas refused. Matheson thought for a moment. John McIver and Donald McAuley had suggested to the judge on Monday that it would be easier if the troops stopped their patrols. Could this be done? This could be done, agreed Dugas, providing he was able to contact the patrols, leaving Matheson and his friends something less than twelve hours to find Morrison.

The Megantic storekeeper, along with McIver and McAuley, two members of the Defense Organization, headed immediately for Scotstown where they borrowed a handcar from Donald McAuley's cousin Murdoch McAuley (a lineman with the Canadian Pacific Railway) and trundled east down the tracks. Dugas had them followed and later wrote the lineman's name in his notebook. As an afterthought, he added Donald McAuley's and John McIver's.

With only minutes left before the Tuesday midnight deadline expired, word reached Gould that Morrison had been found and was agreeable to the terms of the truce. Dugas was pleased. It gave him breathing space before Premier Mercier and his cabinet in Montreal would be at him again. He then summoned Bissonette and his aides, outlining the terms. These, he said with calculated coldness, must not be leaked to the press or he would personally slit someone's throat.

The details were simple. The meeting was set for Thursday afternoon, April 11, with him, Dugas, leaving Gould in John McIver's buggy at 2:30 P.M. There would be *no* police escort. Dugas could see a certain danger in going alone, but there was no alternative. As for the truce, it would be in effect from noon Wednesday, April 10, until 4 A.M. Friday, April 12. Under no circumstances would Morrison be shot at, captured, or bothered during the truce. The rendezvous wasn't divulged, even to the judge.

Peter Spanyaardt found himself back up the same old tree. The Montreal *Star* liked his coverage of the Morrison affair, but felt that one major ingredient was lacking: another interview with Morrison. He was, after all, the central figure in the drama. Spanyaardt, however, had found it increasingly difficult to find anyone to talk to from the Defense Organization, especially since the weekend.

Early Wednesday morning Spanyaardt set off once again from Gould in pursuit of the elusive Morrison. He found the situation curiously quiet. At Marsden, Allardice told him that Carpenter, McMahon, and Leroyer hadn't gone out on their early morning patrol and were at present playing euchre in their tent. This seemed to confirm Spanyaardt's suspicions. A truce was either imminent or in progress. Then why hadn't Malcolm Matheson or Hugh Leonard been in touch with him? He thought a little further. Maybe they were themselves busy looking for Morrison to let him know of the truce. Dugas and Malcolm Matheson had been together Sunday night, and if a truce had been agreed upon, Donald Morrison would obviously have to know. The place to be at this moment then was back in Gould where he could keep an eye on the judge. With a hurried good-by, Spanyaardt climbed aboard his rented horse and wheeled it around for Gould.

Gould, at four o'clock in the afternoon, looked as if school had just been let out. As he rode into the village, soldiers and police were lounging about the main street. They spilled out of the small shops and jammed the hotel bars. Spanyaardt didn't like it. A reporter on the outside of a story was no reporter at all, and he didn't know where to turn.

Help was to arrive from an unexpected source—the editorial offices of the Montreal *Star*. Stepping into the lobby of McCoy's Hotel the desk clerk handed him a telegram dated 1 P.M., Wednesday, April 10.

Sore and bruised from his ride, Peter jammed the unopened telegram deep into his pocket and headed for his room. This was no time for the *Star* to scream about a Morrison interview. He could see the editors leaping about the office calling Spanyaardt a lax, unreliable dolt. Why hadn't he filed an interview? Hadn't he boasted *in print* of being on intimate terms with the outlaw? Spanyaardt reached his room, sat on the bed, and stared down at the paper as his fingers unfolded it. In a partially coded message he was told to leave Gould as inconspicuously as possible and high-tail it for Marsden to await further instructions. He'd have to catch the train at Scotstown.

Spanyaardt heard the anxious hoots of the train far across the countryside as he topped the rise and caught sight of Scotstown spread out below him in the valley. With a shout and a wave of his arms he coaxed his horse into a final gallop, clinging gamely to saddle and mane.

The engine was breaking into the station as the reporter clattered over the bridge by the mill and swung the horse back toward the station. It was after 6:15 P.M. The train tooted its intention of leaving. Spanyaardt dismounted in a flurry of arms, legs, and rearing horse, snapped the reins around the hitch rail and dashed for the nearest coach. He hit the stoop as the engine jerked the cars ahead. Spanyaardt barely had time to yell at the startled stationmaster to water his horse—he'd be back—when the train cleared the village and thundered down the tracks.

At Marsden, Peter Spanyaardt found a local resident waiting for him on the platform. He was asked to identify himself, then together they walked to a nearby mill and took a long walk into the woods. Finally he was left alone. Within thirty minutes a buggy appeared with Donald Morrison in it.

As they shook hands Spanyaardt noticed the change in Morrison since their last meeting. The strength and determination were still there, but his face was thinner and his forehead creased with worry. The famed Megantic Outlaw looked older than his thirty-one years.

Morrison confirmed that the truce had begun at noon that day, Wednesday. But he still didn't trust the police and had made arrangements for this interview through the *Star*'s head office. Morrison then told the reporter about the meeting with Dugas set for the next day, but he gave Spanyaardt no details.

For the next fifteen minutes they talked about those who had been sent to jail; a petty way of dealing with things, Morrison said. There was a strong possibility that the talk with Dugas would prove fruitless. Either way, Donald wouldn't give himself up. Spanyaardt then asked him what feelings he had toward the police. This prompted a grin. He had nothing against them as individuals, Morrison said, because they were only doing their job. The detectives were a different matter. It was they who recently visited his parents' home and broke open Donald's trunk, removing some correspondence. "I wouldn't have cared for other letters, but they might have left my love letters [from Augusta]. I was perfectly stunned when I slipped home and found them gone. Besides, they are simply out for blood money. I do not trust them. I do not trust the truce." Other letters were also removed.

The interview was over. They shook hands and walked back to the buggy. Though it appeared Morrison had come alone, Spanyaardt sensed others about. Once in the buggy Donald turned to him and asked a favor: would Spanyaardt hold back details of this interview till Friday's paper, so nothing would

jeopardize the Dugas meeting tomorrow? Spanyaardt understood
and gave his word. This pleased Morrison, who then promised
he would make sure the reporter was given details of the meeting with Dugas as soon as possible. They shook hands again and
a moment later the buggy was gone.

As darkness closed in, Spanyaardt stood motionless, listening
to unseen figures move away through the wood. Finally he took
a deep breath and looked about him. Only then did he realize he
was lost.

Judge Aimée Dugas leaned his elbows on the chest of
drawers Thursday afternoon and stared at the telegram for a full
ten seconds. From behind he heard the springs of the bed twang
as the expedition's clerk, J. G. Tremblay, shifted impatiently. The
judge was late already, and Dr. Tremblay had been trying to
persuade him to leave before Malcolm Matheson and his crowd
became impatient and dropped the whole business. Dugas, however, was enjoying himself. Sherbrooke must be in one hell of a
state, he thought, with all those Scots in custody. The sender was
J. Sidney Broderick, a lawyer whose name was only slightly familiar to him. Broderick was asking the judge to authorize bail
for his clients, three Scots Dugas had arrested early in his campaign to capture the Megantic Outlaw. Money for their bonds
was also ready, if he would act upon it.

Judge Dugas, however, was not ready. This telegram was
only one of many he had received from lawyers requesting bail
for their clients jailed under the same circumstances. He had ignored those as he would this one. There was no chance at all he
would give bail to anyone, at least until he had met with Morrison this afternoon. Then he changed his mind. If he wired
Broderick, the other dozen lawyers or so would hear about it.
Lawyers were like that. So he told his clerk to send off a wire to
Sherbrooke saying "No." He knew Tremblay's reply, as always,
would be more diplomatic.

No matter how it was taken, the judge was merely stalling for
time, as Tremblay well knew. Dugas now told him outright that
Broderick and the other lawyers involved would then apply for
a writ of *habeas corpus* because the accused had been held for

eight days already without any kind of formal charge being laid against them. The door closed; Tremblay was alone. He thought for a moment, then bent over to write.

GOULD, QUE, APRIL 11, 1889

TO: J. S. BRODERICK: JUDGE DUGAS WILL BE AT SHERBROOKE TO-MORROW. HE SENDS WORD THAT HE WOULD NOT PERMIT THEM TO BAIL NOW IN THEIR [OWN] INTERESTS.

(SIGNED) DR. J. G. TREMBLAY
CLERK TO JUDGE DUGAS

In the lobby below the judge cornered Bissonette, asking him to take care of one small detail, then he stepped outside and walked up the street toward John McIver's waiting buggy. It was 3:45. Dugas was one hour and fifteen minutes late.

Peter Spanyaardt, sitting in a lounge off the lobby, watched Dugas come down the stairway, stop for a word with the high constable, then walk out the front door. All was proceeding well, he thought, settling himself comfortably into the leather-backed chair and closing his eyes. He had spent half the night before finding his way out of the woods near Marsden and the other half writing a brief news report about a "probable" meeting between Dugas and Morrison, then one on his own interview, requesting a "hold" on it till Friday's paper. He wired along with these stories a full explanation.

By this time it was almost dawn on Thursday and he wandered across the way to McLeod's Hotel and roused C. B. Allardice out of a deep sleep. After a lengthy breakfast together, he caught the morning train back to Scotstown to find his horse had been well looked after. From there he rode leisurely back to Gould, and at this precise moment, after Dugas had left the hotel, he had all but persuaded himself to forsake the chair and go upstairs for a sleep when the lobby suddenly exploded with shouts and running feet.

Opening his eyes, he saw Bissonette, followed by at least a dozen police and soldiers, charging out the door. Caught up in the excitement, he too leaped for the door and came to a sliding halt in the middle of the street. Something had gone wrong. To the west, Bissonette was leading a full charge, while to the east, behind him, he caught a glimpse of Judge Dugas disappearing around a corner in a buggy. A ruse, that's what it was, a ruse to keep attention away from the direction Dugas was going. Well, he'd follow neither, although it was rather interesting to see Bissonette was still moving down the street at the gallop. But he'd have to give the high constable credit for such an energetic distraction.

Back in the lobby a few minutes later, Spanyaardt was to find another sort of distraction to keep him occupied: Constable Summerville, of the expeditionary force.

Summerville, on loan from the Quebec provincial police, a large, affable man, took Spanyaardt aside and asked him if he intended going anywhere. Rather indignant, the reporter held his ground. What would the constable do, should he attempt to go anywhere? The constable's face showed a momentary concern. "I'd prevent you from going," he said.

Spanyaardt shrugged. "Then I am under arrest?"

Summerville didn't know quite how to answer. Finally he nodded, saying, "Well, somewhat to that effect."

To Spanyaardt this meant arrest, being detained in his hotel room and not allowed to go anywhere. And Constable Summerville was there to make sure he didn't.

For almost an hour the two men in the buggy didn't speak; Judge Dugas because his mind was too preoccupied with the coming events, John McIver because he'd be damned if he'd make idle talk with a man who had already arrested many of his kith and kin. McIver wasn't at all sure that Dugas wasn't using this meeting to trap Morrison. The Defense Organization had done everything possible to ensure Morrison's safety, but one could never tell. McIver had little faith in these policemen. And beside him was the man responsible for the whole damn mess.

As for Judge Aimée Dugas, he knew he was risking a great deal, putting his safety on the line. Nor was he overjoyed at the prospect of meeting the outlaw on his own ground, under his own terms. He had come with nothing to trade, merely to ask the young man to give himself up. He had been equipped with *no* bargaining power, such as a promise of leniency at the trial. No favors, no promises.

Donald Morrison had chosen for the rendezvous the old log schoolhouse perched atop the Big Hill, a height of land where the Galson road cut south toward McLeod's Crossing. From here the countryside breaks away on all sides, giving a clear view in all directions. At this moment he was watching a lonely buggy coming along the road from Gould. That it kept coming at all was a good sign, for if anything had been amiss, the men guarding the road would have stopped it and signaled danger. When the buggy was within a hundred yards, Morrison spoke briefly to his friends, then went inside.

The others moved aside and Dugas stepped into the schoolhouse. As his eyes became accustomed to the half-light, he found himself facing a man larger than he had expected. Saying nothing, he looked him over carefully; this was the notorious outlaw who'd played his hand like an experienced gambler. Quite suddenly Dugas' feelings went out to this man and he stepped forward, pushing his hand out before him.

Then the room cleared and he was alone with Morrison. Dugas sat down at one of the small desks. Without preliminaries he asked Morrison to quit before blood was shed on both sides. He couldn't win, the judge stated with conviction. It could only lead to more arrests and Morrison would be hunted day and night until brought in dead or alive. Dugas paused, adding that he hadn't come to barter.

Donald smiled grimly. Neither had he. He would surrender only when the judge gave his word that all charges against him and all the Scots were dropped. The judge opened his mouth to speak, but Morrison cut him off, saying on the other hand he was willing to leave the country if Major McAulay gave him the $900. He would then need three days to get away.

The schoolroom became strangely silent. The two men's eyes locked together, with neither giving in. Finally it was the judge who spoke. There was nothing more to say, he said, getting to his feet. Without another word he shook hands and turned abruptly to the door.

It was 8:30 in the evening when he reached McCoy's Hotel. He stepped down from the buggy and, without acknowledging McIver, stepped quickly inside. Bissonette was immediately at his elbow. Seeing the taut, colorless face and dull eyes he sensed the verdict. Without so much as turning his head Dugas ordered the high constable to have all sleighs and wagons available and every man at the ready. They would however respect the 4 A.M. deadline tomorrow, Friday. As he started for the stairway, he glanced at Bissonette and without expression told him that at first light the forty-five additional warrants would be served on those known for "aiding and abetting" one Donald Morrison.

11

DUGAS AND CO.

APRIL 1889

Friday noon, April 12, Judge Aimée Dugas, needing a few days' rest, caught the train for Montreal. Forty-five more warrants were being served and, as he told reporters in Gould, "My presence was no more imperatively required, as the constables have the necessary warrants in hand and everything is in shape to keep them busy. . . ."

And busy the constables were. By Saturday afternoon the police were well on their way to rounding up those listed on the warrants, including William Matheson, the Winslow blacksmith, long a suspected Morrison supporter. High Constable Adolphe Bissonette had discovered letters from the blacksmith to Donald Morrison in the trunk in his parents' home. These traced the movements of the police in their search for the outlaw.

To both Dugas and Bissonette this was a revelation. Not until the discovery of this cache did either realize to what extent the Morrison Defense Organization had developed its communication system. The mail service was one method they police had totally overlooked; with the co-operation of various postmasters, the whereabouts of the police could be traced with ease.

As he had been expecting for several days, Murdoch McAuley, the Canadian Pacific lineman, found himself herded into custody along with four others from the Marsden area. It was Saturday, April 13.

By Monday, however, not all the forty-five warrants had been served. Many of those listed had decided to further complicate the policemen's lot by not being available when the authorities came to their homes to arrest them. They had gone to live with friends or relatives until the way was legally clear for them to return. This came by eleven o'clock in the morning when J. Sidney Broderick managed to file for a writ of *habeas corpus*, making further arrests difficult and at the same time putting pressure on the authorities to release those who had been detained in jail for an inordinate length of time. Irked by the manipulations of the judge, though acting legally for only three of those detained, Broderick argued that eight days was the *longest* period a man could be committed for examination unless some definite grounds were found for further commitment. Most of the imprisoned Scots had been in jail far longer than eight days, as it was, without any formal charges being laid. Bail is only refused, he said firmly, on the most serious of charges, such as murder, and he concluded by saying there was a very fine line between prosecution and persecution. With suspension of further warrants, the Scots at last found a moment to get their second wind.

Pierre Charbonneau hunched his shoulders against the night air. For the first time in weeks the weather had shown no signs of dampness, and now, as he stood on his porch a field or two away from the village of Stornoway, it was giving way to a cool breeze from the west. It was Tuesday, April 16. At noon the temperature had climbed almost to the sixties and everyone around Leonard's Hotel had been in an expansive mood. The first sign of spring always had that effect, especially after a bitterly cold winter. After *any* winter, for that matter; and little work had been accomplished about the hotel. His job as the general handyman at Leonard's still left Charbonneau time enough to operate his own farm. Now, close to ten o'clock, he breathed in deeply and, deciding on the spur of the moment to have a last look around his buildings, stepped off the porch and headed for the stable.

The cattle stirred momentarily as the door creaked open. The barn was also peaceful. He stepped along the planking which

had once been piled high with hay. Now it was desolate. As the
French Canadian walked back toward the door he thought he
saw a movement in the granary. Curious he moved closer and
suddenly found himself face to face with Donald Morrison. The
outlaw's body was outlined in a trace of moonlight which had
found its way between the pine boards of the walls. Stunned,
Charbonneau gawked awkwardly for a moment, caught himself,
then asked if the visitor was hungry. Morrison said no, but
thanked him.

Charbonneau turned and left the barn as quiet as he had
found it, realizing with relief that the rumors he heard at the
hotel that afternoon, about the outlaw being trapped in a
mineshaft at Black Lake were completely unfounded. On his
way back to the house the French Canadian chuckled at the hell
it would raise if he stopped off at the hotel and informed Sub-
Chief Lancy and his men that Donald Morrison was resting in
his barn. They'd only tell him he was seeing ghosts.

At the same moment, High Constable Adolphe Bissonette in
Gould would undoubtedly have given his right arm to be privy
to Morrison's whereabouts. For once he figured he had Morrison
where he wanted him—deep in a copper mine, with only one
exit. And how he had wished to present Dugas with the captive
outlaw, when the judge returned tomorrow from Montreal.

Word had come into Gould that morning that three men had
been seen descending a mine near Black Lake, sixty miles to the
north, and one had been identified as Donald Morrison. The idea
caught Bissonette's imagination.

Captains Giroux and Haigham were put on to the story immediately. They found the source of this information to be a
Montreal lawyer, J. N. Greenshields, Q.C., who was up visiting
his mining interests. Yes, others too had seen Morrison in the vicinity.

By eleven that Tuesday morning Bissonette and a hand-
picked crew of ten, headed by Giroux and Haigham, had arrived
at Black Lake aboard a coach of the Quebec Central Railway
and were promptly met by Excelsior Copper Company executive
Georges Prideaux. After introducing himself, he took the party
directly to the Harvey mineshaft. Bissonette would later recall

the stirrings of triumph he felt as they descended 1,600 feet below the surface, a stirring which no doubt helped offset his claustrophobia. This expectant triumph faded over the next eight hours as the force combed every inch of the Harvey mine, then repeated the search in neighboring Kent and Fanny Eliza shafts, only to come away with nothing but coughs, running noses, and ringing ears.

Greenshields the lawyer had already gone back to Sherbrooke, but once the story was straightened out, it seemed he had asked in Blacks Lake about news of Morrison and someone had thought he had seen him, none of which impressed Bissonette. He had never felt more discouraged about the entire search as he did on the train ride back to Weedon. It hurt him more to admit to himself that if Dugas had been here, *he* wouldn't have gone off on such a wild search. The judge would have seen at once that no man on the run would go anywhere that led to a dead end. A mineshaft was certainly all of that.

Good Friday, the nineteenth of April. Judge Dugas had come back through Sherbrooke, settled matters with the lawyers, permitting those jailed to be released on bail, and continued on to Gould. Awaiting him were members of the local Caledonian Society, a nonprofit organization which promoted good will and brotherhood among Scots everywhere. So said the Reverend C. J. McLeod, a Presbyterian minister from nearby Marsboro, who introduced his friends, Dr. J. H. Graham, chief of the Caledonian chapter in Richmond, and Captain Norman Nicholson, also of Richmond. They had come to express their opinion that the only way of ending this travesty of a manhunt was once more through negotiations. To this purpose, they told Judge Dugas, they had met with Premier Mercier and other Quebec parliamentary figures, suggesting a second meeting between the judge and Morrison under the auspices of the Caledonian Society. Graham and Nicholson had brought certain letters with them, one from the Honorable Edward Blake, a member of the Quebec parliament and prominent figure in the Scottish movement, urging Donald Morrison to accept terms suggested by the three representatives of the Caledonian Society.

A second letter was the result of a meeting with Premier

Mercier, which, as the judge would see, instructed High Constable Adolphe Bissonette to guarantee a second truce, effective from Saturday, April 20, to Easter Monday evening, April 22, during which time Graham, Nicholson, and McLeod might personally discuss the matter with Donald Morrison and set up a meeting between him and the judge. They hoped, they said, to arrange the meeting for Easter Monday. The matter was settled and the truce terms set, if Morrison didn't object. Satisfied with the co-operation they had received, the three men set out for Stornoway where they would contact members of the Defense Organization and subsequently chat with the outlaw. They could see no problems and would remain at Leonard's Hotel, they decided, for the weekend.

Peter Spanyaardt was among those who greeted them at Leonard's. Knowing little about the Caledonian Society, he asked if their stay had anything to do with Morrison. The question caught them off guard, and after a flustered deliberation, they told him they had no comment at present. Spanyaardt excused himself (not wanting to press them too hard at first) and ordered a second drink. He was celebrating his second interview story with Donald Morrison, which had appeared in that day's edition of the Montreal *Star* along with another story on the same page saying how Spanyaardt had been "arrested" and detained in his hotel room. Both had been well received by his editors. However, he could smell some sort of connection between these new arrivals and Donald Morrison and he would have to press it home later.

Over a nightcap he convinced the three newcomers that he could be of value, letting them know what was transpiring in both camps, in exchange for knowing what their role in all this might be. They discreetly told him all they could, on the promise he would withhold the information for the present.

On his way to breakfast early Saturday morning, Spanyaardt found a message from Allardice waiting for him at the desk. The reporter wanted him to come immediately to Marsden, though he gave no reason. This would upset Spanyaardt's plans; he had wanted to be around when the Caledonian men met Bissonette. However if Allardice said it was urgent. . . .

Borrowing a horse from the hotel, he set out at the gallop. As instructed, Spanyaardt rode directly to the Marsden station. Stepping onto the platform he was amazed to find his friend standing forlornly beside his battered suitcase. Allardice wasn't in a happy frame of mind. He had been recalled to Montreal. Spanyaardt swore aloud. How *could* he be? Allardice answered with a shrug of his shoulders, saying he had received the message early this morning. He was being recalled because word had reached the *Star* that Judge Dugas would be spending Easter in Montreal, along with Bissonette. With them both away from the Eastern Townships, there would be little sense having two reporters on the Morrison job. Spanyaardt raised his arms in a gesture of hopelessness, letting them drop to his sides. Suddenly he wondered what sort of games the members of the Caledonian Society were playing.

Allardice was looking at him strangely. Was there something wrong? Spanyaardt said he didn't know. Probably not. Allardice waited for a moment. When his friend didn't speak, he added that everyone seemed on edge this morning. Was it some sort of conspiracy? Spanyaardt passed it off with a laugh. What did he mean? Allardice grinned. He had bumped into McMahon, Carpenter and Leroyer this morning and they seemed as jumpy as ticks. The only piece of information he could get from them was that, in the absence of Dugas and Bissonette, Captain Giroux would be in charge. Spanyaardt shrugged and reached out to give his friend a pat on the shoulder. They had worked well together. It didn't seem right to split the team up only to save a few dollars—and besides it wasn't the proper time to have only one reporter here. He was about to mention Graham when the sounds of an approaching train interrupted him.

Peter Spanyaardt found a less than buoyant chief of the Caledonian Society, Richmond Chapter, when he arrived back at Leonard's Hotel in Stornoway shortly before noon on Saturday. Graham met him in the lobby and asked him in strict confidence to divulge no news about the proceedings. Spanyaardt chortled aloud. Didn't the doctor realize his proceedings had fallen apart? Dugas and Bissonette were heading home and he . . . Graham cut him off with a sudden laugh. *All* was arranged, he said, taking the reporter by the elbow and leading him out onto the veranda. Of course, he knew about Dugas and Bissonette heading for Montreal—but not before all had been settled. The truce would begin that morning and last until Monday night when a meeting had been scheduled. News of the meeting would be announced in the churches on Sunday. On *Easter* Sunday, imagine!

But Spanyaardt didn't like the smell of it. These Caledonians, he thought to himself over lunch, were being duped *somewhere*, and for the life of him he couldn't think how. It was perfectly reasonable that Dugas and Bissonette wanted to be with their families for Easter, but only if the meeting was set for Monday. And yet so far, Dugas' "expedition" hadn't really been at all successful. Surely Premier Mercier was aware of it and was applying pressure. Men don't blithely take off under these circumstances. No, damn it, something was wrong. If only Graham and his little troop showed a little less credulity, it would be one hell of a lot better.

The notion that something far deeper was unfolding plagued Peter Spanyaardt. Allardice's remark about Carpenter being edgy bothered him. Captain Giroux was another question. Why had he been left in charge, if little would be happening before Easter Monday? Why didn't they *all* go home, for God's sake? Graham had all but *told* him the meeting would be on Easter Monday.

At supper Saturday evening, Spanyaardt joined Dr. Graham and Captain Nicholson at the table by the window. Dr. McLeod had excused himself and returned to his parish in Marsboro to prepare for the Easter services.

Graham was now in an expansive mood. He praised the thick barley soup and helped himself to a third scone, which, he claimed, had been cooked the way all scones should be cooked, on the griddle. Spanyaardt didn't share his enthusiasm, but enjoyed the Scottish oat bread and ate more of his share of the *tourtières*, with stovies and fresh dandelion greens. He had hoped to learn more about plans for the meeting, but didn't want to mix business with pleasure. He watched as Graham eyed the maple-sugar pie.

Though he pressed Graham for further details about the Dugas-Morrison meeting over coffee, the Caledonian man just shook his head, saying finally that Spanyaardt wasn't to worry, he'd get a good story in the end. That, he said with a benevolent smile, he could promise.

Chief Detective Silas Carpenter stretched his legs flat out along the only piece of grass he could find, shifted his posterior from one side to the other till he found some degree of comfort, and leaned against the rock behind him. This Godforsaken country, he murmured as he looked around him. This morning the ground oozed mud and the air hung thick with moisture. It would undoubtedly start raining again, as it had all night.

Easter. Easter Sunday. God bless. All good families nestled in their warm beds or eating breakfasts by the fire, Dugas and Bissonette included. And here he was, sitting in the middle of nowhere while his two companions snored a duet in the sodden tent behind him. Well, they wouldn't be here much longer anyway; any of them. And that suited Silas Carpenter just fine.

Bissonette had sent for him around 4 A.M. Saturday, several hours before the high constable caught the train for Montreal. When the chief detective arrived at Leonard's Hotel in Stornoway, he found Bissonette pacing the lobby, alone. After a short exchange about the nasty weather, the high constable had led Carpenter into a far corner of the darkened lounge.

It was then that Bissonette told Silas Carpenter what was to take place over the next forty-eight hours. Carpenter, startled at first, listened intently to what was expected of him. He nodded, made some suggestions and wondered grimly to himself if Bissonette realized the gravity of the plan.

Shortly after six o'clock they stood up and shook hands. Carpenter asked if extra men could be sent to his tent camp opposite the elder Morrison's log home. Bissonette said he would take care of it, before he left.

Carpenter had returned immediately. Waking up McMahon and Leroyer, he told them precisely what Bissonette had said. By noon Saturday, Constables Albert McKeown and Henry Gordon arrived, leaving later to sleep over in Spring Hill.

The vigil, already twenty-four hours old, had produced nothing. It was Sunday morning now. Six A.M. The moment McKeown and Gordon returned, Silas Carpenter, under previous orders, would take up his post in Stornoway.

Across the fields in the small log house, Murdo and Sophia Morrison couldn't sleep that morning either. They both puttered aimlessly about, hardly exchanging glances, let alone words. Time was heavy on their hands, heavier still on their hearts. Winter had taken its toll of their energies and today, Easter Sunday, they were trying to fill the excruciatingly long moments before Donald would come again. He had promised. Besides, it was Easter. This time he would come without fear of capture. Sophia knew that she hadn't many Easters left.

Their daughter Christie MacArthur, from down the road, had rushed over last night to tell them about the truce. It would be announced in church today, but she'd heard it from the stationmaster who heard it from . . . well, she wasn't sure who *he* got it from. Sophia and Murdo had looked at each other with quiet apprehension. Maybe this truce would be different. Maybe. . . . Anyway, he'd come to see them today and she would make a point of having him change into better clothes and have a shave, to look nice for Easter. They had looked after his best gray suit. It was already spread out for him on the couch in the corner.

Though the rainy weather failed to improve at all on Easter Sunday, it didn't dampen the spirits of local parishioners who filled the houses of worship from St. Agnes in Megantic to the small wood-frame churches scattered about the community in places like Marsboro, Tolsta, Gould, and North Hill. And along with solemn thanksgiving, the congregations heard the news that the Caledonian Society had arranged a truce for Donald Morrison and a second meeting tomorrow between him and Judge Dugas. It came as a happy surprise. Having the "prisoners" back from jail had already made it an unusually joyous occasion.

For Donald Morrison, Easter was hardly a day to celebrate. The truce, which he had learned about the night before at Tolsta, would force him to give in, a little at least. He wondered what the men from the Caledonian Society had in mind. Surely they realized he wouldn't submit to Dugas' present terms of "no guarantees." Maybe they had already talked to the judge and come up with new terms? It was this possibility that prompted Morrison to agree to meet with Dr. Graham, sending back the message that he would be in Stornoway Easter night. In the meantime, he wanted to be on his own, to come to terms with the latest developments.

Facing up to these random thoughts this Easter morning gave Donald Morrison a long-needed feeling of release. He wished Augusta and Norman MacAulay were there to brighten his moments of solitude. He had awakened early in a barn near Spring Hill, to find himself lying on a small patch of hay left from winter feed. He came to the bemused conclusion—a fact he would gratuitously pass on to all would-be outlaws—that fall and winter were the best times of the year to be on the run; the barns were full of hay, making sleep far more comfortable. The dearth of such bedding in spring made negotiations with his hunters seem almost inevitable.

Pulling on his boots, Morrison left the barn and headed directly for the woods. While washing in the first stream he came to, he decided that Easter would be a time for visiting friends he'd long neglected. But he wouldn't yet be so bold as to show himself along the main thoroughfares. Some trigger-happy bounty hunter might take a shot at him regardless of the truce, claiming later he hadn't been told.

By early evening Donald had visited half a dozen homes where he was greeted with genuine affection and much happiness. His spirits were lifted, and he joined in the lively conversations centered mainly on past times. Everyone insisted on his staying for a meal. Before the day was little more than half over he was already stuffed to bursting with barley bread, succulent meats, potatoes, buckwheat cakes, and hot scones. When he was ready to move on, someone always insisted on accompanying him, but he begged to go alone, not wishing to take them from their families on a day like Easter.

Dusk was shrouding the countryside when Donald stepped from the woods north of his mother and father's home. He paused for a moment, looking over at Murdo Murray's farm. He thought of borrowing a horse from Murdo for the journey later to Stornoway, but anxious to see his parents, he headed directly for the log house.

Constable James McMahon and guide Pierre Leroyer had few shared interests. Both had independently come to the same

Donald Morrison's father, Murdo, stands before the log cabin near Marsden where Donald was captured. Number 1 marks where McMahon and Leroyer were hiding when Morrison emerged from the cabin door. Number 2 marks where Morrison fell over the fence and was captured. (Photo, J. A. Jones)

The Sherbrooke courthouse where Donald Morrison's trial took place in October 1889. The actual courtroom windows are those with white blinds along the second story. Today the building is used as an armory by the Sherbrooke Hussars. (Photo, Clarke Wallace)

John Leonard, one of Morrison's defense lawyers and a family friend.

J. N. Greenshields, chief counsel for the defense. (Photo, Canada Wide)

L. C. Belanger, one of the lawyers for the Crown. (Photo, Canada Wide)

Justice Edward Tearle Brooks, who presided at Donald Morrison's trial (Photo, Canada Wide)

Photos and sketches used by *The World Wide Magazine* for an article about the Megantic Outlaw in one of its 1912 issues. The article was written by Peter Spanyaardt, though he cut down his byline to read "Peter Span." Leading figures in the drama, in the photos at the right, are shown as they looked in 1912.

This wreath was placed on Donald Morrison's grave in the Guisla Cemetery by the Caledonian Society.

conclusion that the best way of getting along together was to remain silent. This they did with great success, exchanging glances only when a need arose for communication.

With Carpenter gone and McKeown and Gordon haunting the nearby woods, McMahon glanced at Leroyer hunched down by the fire, then moved away to sit beneath some bushes, in the vain hope of getting out of the rain. It didn't work, but he sat there anyway, peeved that the Frenchman across the way seemed oblivious to the miserable conditions which had them soaked to their skins.

By late afternoon McMahon told Gordon and McKeown to take shelter in the tent. He'd call if they were needed. He caught the relief on their faces and turned abruptly away. With a nod to Leroyer they shuffled off through the wet grass toward a pile of logs which had been piled carelessly by the side of the road. Once again they huddled down, making sure they had a clear view of the small log cabin across the field, a hundred yards away.

An hour later their patience was rewarded. Leroyer saw him first, partially lost in the gathering ground fog. He was beside the barn. Leroyer nudged the constable.

"Morrison?" whispered McMahon.

Leroyer wasn't sure. He watched the figure move casually away from the frame barn and move toward the log house, pause, then walk to the door facing them. A second later he disappeared inside. It could easily have been Morrison, Leroyer thought, a smile building up on his thin lips.

Now McMahon wasn't absolutely sure. He suggested they'd better wait, moving up for a closer look when it became darker. Leroyer was not waiting for anything. Without a word he slipped around the pile of wood and struck out for the road, bent well over as he ran. When he was a dozen paces of the only window in the cabin, he dropped down behind the thick pole fence and waited until a lamp was lit inside. Only then did he cautiously approach for a better look at the visitor. Within five minutes a grinning Pierre Leroyer confirmed to McMahon that Donald Morrison was indeed inside the log house.

For an hour James McMahon and Pierre Leroyer pressed themselves against the wall of the Morrison barn, with their rifles, safety catches off, clutched, and ready. They waited, nerves raw, eyes fastened on a spot where the logs came together at the end of the house.

Leroyer didn't like the spot McMahon had selected. Neither could see the front of the house or the only door. What if Morrison came and turned *left* instead of coming this way, as he had come? He'd be gone in an instant. Leroyer snarled. McMahon said it was a chance they'd have to take. If they were out front, sure as hell the outlaw would start shooting the moment he knew he was trapped and their returning gunfire might endanger the man's parents. Leroyer shrugged his sodden shoulders. He for one wouldn't press the trigger till the outlaw was well clear of the door. But, insisted McMahon, if Morrison ducked to the right, around this corner, he'd be out of their range in a second. Leroyer didn't agree. Why didn't they split up, he said sarcastically, and get into each other's line of fire?

McMahon saw no humor in the remark. He shifted his back hard against the barn, taking some of the weight off his legs which were bent under him. They were numb, so he leaned to one side, straightened one leg, then shifted the other way, dropping his weary butt down onto the soft moist earth. Leroyer was right and McMahon knew it. Lose Morrison this time and his promotion, if not his job, would go out the goddamn window. Morrison was wanted for murder, alive or bloody well dead. Dugas would accept no excuse. Neither would Police Chief Hughes in Montreal or the premier, for Christ's sake, so he'd better get to the best location where he could do the most damage or he would lose everything.

Besides, never in all his years on the force, never through the stake-outs, shootings, near-deaths, triumphs, and despairs had he ever wanted to capture one man as badly as he did Morrison. He was thirsty for Morrison, a thirst which went far beyond a physical dryness. He wanted Morrison and nothing would prevent him getting him. Absolutely nothing, he said to himself, nudging Leroyer in the ribs.

Moving in close, McMahon could smell the musky deadness of Leroyer's sodden leather jacket, stale tobacco, the sweet and sour scent of his wet skin. They would swing wide past the barn, McMahon whispered hoarsely, over to the road, then up along the pole fence and stop short of the house. Without waiting for a reply, the constable scrambled to his feet and with a crablike motion scuttled out past the barn and disappeared into the darkness. Leroyer held back momentarily, then followed.

Within minutes they had dropped down in the mud on the far side of the fence, placing it between themselves and the log house. Crawling now on hands and knees, their rifles cradled across their elbows, they moved forward until the east corner of the cabin was no more than a dozen paces away. This put the only door at the other end, diagonally across from them.

Both men were now completely oblivious to anything around them, save the window and the door beyond. Sprawled flat out in the wet mud, their bodies lying parallel to the pole fence, each had tugged his Colt revolver free from their encumbering clothes and set it against the lowest pole, within easy reach. The barrels of their rifles protruded between the poles, aimed in the general direction of the house.

No sooner had they settled down when a shadow passed the window. McMahon grasped Leroyer by the shoulder, at the same time ducking. Had someone inside caught movement in the yard? When he looked up the curtainless window was empty.

This window itself was some ten feet to the right of the door. The door too wasn't part of the log house, but rather formed a portion of a roofed lean-to attached directly to the left side of the building. The constable knew this was the woodshed with a second door leading into the house. Morrison would step first into this shed before opening the outer door. His mother and father would probably remain inside when saying good-by. Bissonette had been correct so far. With any luck he might be correct all the way.

It was almost nine.

Inside the log house Donald changed into his good clothes, stood quietly searching his father's face for some show of emotion. He found it in the still-glistening eyes. Suddenly Donald's mouth bent into the old familiar grin and father and son reached out, bringing their arms tightly around each other.

Murdo held on tenaciously, feeling the strength in hands and arms ebbing as his emotions thundered within him. Sobs soon began wracking his body as the years of doubt and self-recrimination gathered like a storm. It was only when Sophia gently wrapped her arms about him that Murdo's body lost its will and he hung onto her as he'd never done before.

For uncounted minutes the three stood close, dispelling the years of heartache and distrust. It was Donald who finally wrenched himself free, turning away to wipe his tears with the palms of his hands. A moment later Sophia loaded his arms with a blanket and a small parcel of food. Now she too was holding him close, repeating over and over *"Na imich a mach an nockd a Dhomhnull."* (Don't go out tonight, Donald.) Donald finally eased her back, saying, *"'S fheadar dhomh a mhathair"* (I must go, mother), and he reached back with his free hand and opened the door.

As he stepped into the shed, he felt his father close behind him. Donald took three steps forward, stopped at the outer door and looked back at his parents' tear-stained faces. He put his hand out seizing the leather thong on the door. He pulled it toward him. The door was stuck. He pulled again, and the door swung inward. *"Beannachd leibh,"* he whispered and stepped into the night.

Leroyer saw him first. McMahon, having glanced down to check the catch on his Colt, heard Leroyer suddenly suck in his breath. He looked up to see Donald Morrison in the doorway, his face turned, looking back. He was carrying something under his right arm, but it wasn't a rifle.

Both men held their breaths, watching Morrison hesitate, then step forward. Time slowed to a crawl as they saw him move away from the house and start in their direction.

Leroyer's hand tightened on the butt of his revolver. His mind screamed within him and his mouth went bone dry. McMahon's hand moved across the other man's revolver holding him back, a little longer. Directly over Morrison's left shoulder McMahon could see the faded outline of the old man's head.

Morrison's face showed no expression as he moved quietly alongside the house. Halfway between door and fence, either the blanket or parcel must have slipped, for he made a sudden duck-

ing motion, bringing his left hand up from under to support
them. The move hadn't been completed when McMahon and
Leroyer leveled their revolvers and fired simultaneously.

The sound of exploding .45s racketed off the log building and
resounded out across the empty fields. Bits of wood, torn away
by the impact of the slugs, shot crazily into the air as Donald
threw himself forward, still unsure from which direction the bullets had been fired. As he ducked down he dug his free hand into
his waistband, tugging frantically at the butt of his own revolver.

They had caught him completely off guard, but his reflexes,
by now attuned to any surprise, jerked him forward as his legs
drove him past the corner of the house and into the field. More
shots rang out. Donald threw his body from side to side trying to
make himself as difficult a target as possible. Just ahead now he
saw the blurred outlines of the large tree root. If he could only
reach it. Ten feet away. He struggled and pitched his way toward it, his mind racing before him. Five feet. Shots screamed
everywhere. He drove his legs deep into the soft earth. As he
leaped forward, a cacophony of bullets exploded around him. He
seemed to hang suspended in the air before the ground suddenly
rushed up at him.

Donald rolled and pitched along the ground. He felt the bun-
dles ripped from under his right arm, saw a flash of his Colt
clutched tightly in his left hand as he struck the earth again and
skidded to a stop in the mud.

He heard nothing now, just the sound of his own raspy
breathing. He struggled to get up, but his left leg didn't seem
part of him. It was becoming numb as though he'd been stung
by a swarm of angry wasps. His brain awhirl, he groped clumsily
forward, searching for his blanket and parcel, the milk forgotten.
He pulled them in close to his body and still holding his revolver
he struggled to get himself up. Half erect, a hail of shouts and
screams and whining bullets crashed down on him. All at once
his mind became clear. He saw the stump to his right and a
fence beyond. Behind it, he'd stand a chance of saving his own
life.

Moving, stumbling, pitching, Donald propelled himself forward, dragging his left leg behind him. The fence, he knew he

must reach that fence. But the world came to him now in slow
motion. He fought to keep himself upright, spitting at the dirt
which clogged his mouth and filled his eyes.

The fence. Just ahead. But how far? It blurred and moved
before him. His mind had blotted out the sounds of bullets
which were burying themselves in the mud at his feet. It cut the
screams of his mother and father and the shouts of someone
yelling not to let him reach the fence.

The fence. It came up fast. It caught him viciously in the
midsection. He jackknifed forward, the lower portion of his body
coming to an abrupt halt while, curiously, the upper part kept
going on and on, then down and down. The fence. Somehow in
his groggy mind he'd lost its purpose and his shoulders dropped
and his brain turned his world upside down.

Next, his head and shoulders crashed into the poles and
Donald found himself staring up at his legs as they made a lazy
arc against the dark sky. His legs then came down on his chest
and he rolled over once and stopped rolling. He was still. Everything was still. He opened his eyes and heard the lids grating
against dirt lodged between them and the eye sockets. A fence
post, blurred and unrecognizable, leaned against his nose. He
pulled back, listening to voices, angry, muffled, muted voices rising and falling and echoing about him.

He moaned, hearing his own voice gurgling in his throat. The
damn wasps were at him again. Why didn't someone stop them?
Someone did. They snapped his arm back and crunched it down
into the mud. He fumbled for the blanket and the parcel with his
other hand, but they were gone. So he pulled the trigger, but it
was gone.

Something moved beside him. He reached up to push it
away, but they were lying on both arms now. The wasps the
bloody wasps were there too. Tummy down. His face splatted in
the mud which he couldn't breathe. But it didn't matter, because
he knew that he couldn't run any more.

FIVE

CAPTIVE

12

THE LONGEST NIGHT

APRIL–OCTOBER 1889

Dr. J. H. Graham was a nervous wreck. Where was Donald Morrison? He paced the foyer of Leonard's Hotel in Stornoway, periodically removing the watch from the upper pocket of his vest, squinting at it, then jamming it back. The last time he looked it was almost 11 P.M. Seated by the window nearby were Captain Nicholson and Mr. McLeod who shared the doctor's concern in their own way. They chattered incessantly in tones loud enough to make it annoying, too softly to be overheard.

For the past two hours Hugh Leonard and Peter Spanyaardt had been with the Caledonian men, but moments before had gone to the kitchen for some warm milk. Leonard too was anxious about Morrison. He candidly confessed it wasn't like Morrison to let things go like this. He would have come to Stornoway regardless, if only to say he'd changed his mind.

Spanyaardt wished them all goodnight at 11:30 and within half an hour was asleep. An hour later he was awakened by the sound of a galloping horse pulling to a stop below on the street. The reporter sat bolt upright, listening to the heavy boots running across the veranda, and the front door all but rattled off its hinges.

Within seconds the boots came pounding up the staircase and along the corridor, stopping abruptly at the room next to his, occupied by Chief Detective Silas Carpenter. Spanyaardt leaped from his bed and stood pressed against the wall. He heard a short exchange, but it was too muffled to pick up the words. At once the footsteps retreated back down the hall. The next instant it sounded as if Silas Carpenter was in a hurry.

Spanyaardt made a dive in the dark for his own clothes. He had one leg searching frantically for a trouser leg when a door opened, and he heard footsteps running for the stairs. Grabbing his shirt, he opened his door and ran in the opposite direction, to waken Dr. Graham.

The door was ajar. He walked in unannounced. Hugh Leonard was there and a man they called Major McMinn. Lying prostrate on the bed was an ashen-faced Graham. He looked as though he'd aged ten years. McMinn, interrupted by the intrusion, turned back to Graham. "We have been deceived," he said, his voice wavering, "and Morrison has been betrayed during a pretended truce."

Spanyaardt felt his mouth and throat go dry. He swung around to Leonard, speechless. Leonard nodded. "Outside his parents' home," he said, as though not believing it himself.

"When?" snapped Spanyaardt.

"Several hours ago." Leonard then explained about the knocking and finding a courier looking for Carpenter. He had told the lad where he'd be found and on the stairs the courier shouted back how Morrison had been gunned down by McMahon and Leroyer, but was still alive.

Spanyaardt mumbled to himself and was about to leave when Graham moaned. "I will go to Montreal," he wailed softly, "and see Judge Dugas . . . and Premier Mercier." His voice dissolved into a gurgle, but Spanyaardt waited instinctively. "Mr. . . . Bissonette *told* me . . . that if I wanted more time than Monday night to find Morrison . . . I would simply have to wire him. . . ."

Cursing openly, Peter Spanyaardt left the room, stopping long enough to put on his shoes, a sweater, and a coat. Then he stepped quickly into the hallway. As he passed Captain Giroux's room he heard the sounds of heavy breathing. Spanyaardt cursed again.

When the reporter arrived at the Morrison home he was told

by several policemen on guard that the prisoner had been taken to the Marsden station "under heavy guard." Spanyaardt stayed for a few moments to talk to old Murdo Morrison, then raced for the main road leading to Marsden.

The policeman had put it mildly. Marsden was literally crawling with soldiers and police, all armed to the teeth. Tethering his horse to the rail outside the Temperance Hotel, Spanyaardt wasted little time reaching the station.

Security there was exceedingly tight. Within thirty paces of the station, he ground to a halt before two crossed rifles which were pressed unceremoniously against his chest. The faces behind them were unfriendly. He began at once to explain that he was with the press, but the expressions didn't alter. With nothing left to do, Spanyaardt sighed and quite suddenly seized the rifle of the nearest man and pushed with all his might. The soldier, caught completely off guard, stumbled backwards, caught a heel and took his companion with him. By the time they recovered Spanyaardt was lost among the milling crowd.

Though it had taken him five minutes to bull his way to the steps of the station platform, no amount of pushing, shoving, or pure obstinancy got him further. Frustrated and not a little angry, he stood on his toes, frantically looking about for someone who might oblige him with permission to pass. He found such a man coming across the platform: Chief Detective Silas Carpenter who, from his strut and demeanor, was obviously the man in charge. The reporter shouted over the chaos and caught Carpenter's attention, which was enough to get himself onto the platform. He then took aim at the station's waiting room and didn't stop until he was safely inside.

He found Donald Morrison wrapped in rugs and blankets and lying face down on the bare floor. As he moved toward him, Leroyer, standing nearby, put out his hand. He was all right, the guide said, his mouth twisting into an easy smile. Spanyaardt answered that the man quite obviously was not all right, but was told curtly that Morrison chose to lie on his stomach because it was easiest on his wound. Spanyaardt nodded, then asked how many times he had been shot. "Several times," came the answer. The worst shot had been taken in the hip.

Spanyaardt watched as Leroyer brought the back of his hand

across his mouth. His eyes flashed as he recounted how Morrison had started shooting. On the floor Morrison moaned and tried to lift his head. Immediately two police, standing nearby, reached down, pinning him unnecessarily to the floor. The prisoner ignored them. "How can a man tell such things," he yelled. "The Lord Almighty may cut me in two if I ever fired one shot." Spanyaardt's eyes swung from Morrison to Leroyer. The smile had faded. The guide stepped forward, easing the reporter out of the way.

Not wanting to jeopardize an opportunity to talk with Morrison, Peter Spanyaardt stepped aside and found himself listening to Constable McKeown, who had run across from McMahon's camp to the Morrison place the moment the shooting began. McKeown had asked the outlaw later, "Are you wounded?" And Morrison had answered, "Not very badly, but I wish you would take out your revolver and shoot me." McKeown also told the press that Morrison had two revolvers on him, one found still in his waistband; McMahon had taken the other.

Moving about the station more freely now, Spanyaardt came back to Leroyer, who seemed more willing to talk. He told the reporter how he and McMahon had fired at the same time, making it impossible to say which bullet had struck the outlaw. He had heard more shots at the time, thinking they might have come from Morrison, then remembered both McKeown and Gordon. They had been in the camp across the road and had come to their aid. It was news to Spanyaardt that the constables had joined Leroyer and McMahon later that afternoon. He thanked Leroyer and walked away.

The small waiting room was packed with police now, all curiously shifting about, trying to catch a glimpse of Morrison. It was 2:30 A.M. Monday morning, and Spanyaardt, feeling suddenly closed in, stepped onto the platform for a breath of fresh air. A moment later he returned, hoping to have an unguarded moment with Morrison. Walking directly over to the prostrate man he knelt down. The prisoner turned his head, nodded in recognition, then let his head sink back to the bare floor.

The reporter said he had very little time and could Morrison please recall for him exactly what had taken place. Donald obliged as best he could in their few moments together, though he was obviously in great pain. He hadn't quite finished when Spanyaardt felt a hand resting on his shoulder. Carpenter was standing over them. He told the reporter to leave the prisoner alone. Spanyaardt stood up. He asked about the truce, fighting to hold his emotions in control. Carpenter shrugged and turned away. Spanyaardt grabbed his arms asking again. The detective stopped. He sighed and without looking at Spanyaardt said he would only tell him what was happening next. Spanyaardt listened. A special train had been requested to take the prisoner to Sherbrooke. He expected it to arrive from Megantic around 3 A.M., twenty minutes from now.

As Spanyaardt turned away, he could hear Donald call out for a drink. For a moment the crowd went quiet. Then from the middle of the room a young policeman stepped forward, taking a bottle from his pocket. He knelt down beside Morrison, lifted his head gently, and placed the bottle to his lips. It contained a mixture of brandy and water, the policeman told Spanyaardt later, a little something to keep the blood circulating while out on patrol. No one would hazard a night out without his small flask.

The special train arrived three minutes late. Spanyaardt could physically sense the release of tension as many of the expeditionary force climbed aboard. It was feared that Morrison's Defense Organization might make some sort of counterattack, but the fear was never realized. The "spontaneous" capture of Morrison had taken the entire Eastern Townships by surprise.

Morrison was placed aboard one of the coaches, accompanied by an armed guard of fifty men. Carpenter conducted the loading maneuver in his best military manner, then gave orders for the train to be underway. The next stop would be Sherbrooke and jail.

Among the soldiers and police detailed to accompany Morrison, Carpenter found, to his chagrin, Peter Spanyaardt. He would happily have tossed him off, had it not been too late. The detective didn't have the fortitude or effrontery to risk stopping the train in order to rid himself of the reporter.

With the special train's arrival in Sherbrooke shortly before 6 A.M. Donald Morrison was whisked away under heavy guard to the gaunt stone jail on the hill overlooking the town and placed immediately under the care of Dr. F. J. Austin and Dr. N. L. Worthington, both having been warned of the prisoner's arrival. Medical reports showed later that Morrison suffered only one serious wound, that from a .45-caliber slug which tore through the left buttock and egressed from the right hip, traveling a distance of 11½ inches. Spanyaardt, who had maneuvered himself into the jail, wondered how this could be; both the police and old Murdo Morrison claimed Donald's right side should have been exposed to gunfire.

The doctors confirmed the entrance of the bullet into the left buttock. They had also discovered the slug, found in the clothing, which was flattened on the end, indicating it had struck a bone on its way through. Spanyaardt remembered Leroyer claiming he didn't know which of their first shots had struck the outlaw, but it was obvious now that it was a later shot that hit him, possibly when he was tumbling about. Asked about his general condition, the doctors said Morrison was in no danger, but an operation would be necessary to repair damage to the hip bone. They also feared the possibility of orysipeias setting in. Worthington caught Spanyaardt's puzzled look and replaced "orysipeias" with "suppuration," which didn't help. The doctor smiled, saying how the "collecting of pus in the wound" might explain it. Spanyaardt settled for the last explanation.

The reporter then went in search of McMahon and Leroyer who hadn't left Morrison's side since he had been placed on the train at Marsden. They were about to leave the prison when Spanyaardt stopped them for some questions. A few moments later Spanyaardt was seen rushing down to the railway station to wire off the remainder of his story. It would cover almost three columns of that day's Montreal *Star*. It began by boldly declaring Donald Morrison had been captured during a truce.

> . . . Before Mr. Bissonette left for home, he gave Detective Carpenter certain instructions, the purport of which is not known, though it has since been found, through the admissions of Constable McMahon and Pete Leroyer, that they laid in am-

bush for Morrison near his father's
home on the Marsden Road since Saturday night which was done, according to an official, because it was
known that he would come there for
his best clothes, which he would undoubtedly put on in the case of an interview.

The story was complete; Spanyaardt had forgotten nothing,
reporting as best he could the events as they happened. He
knew, as others who read the news report couldn't fail to realize,
that the truce had been a sorry hoax, and through manipulation,
Dugas and Bissonette in Montreal, Carpenter in Stornoway "entertaining" the Caledonian Society, the way had been left open
to capture Donald Morrison by any means possible dead or
alive. McMahon and Leroyer had tried their best to see him
dead. In that, at least, they had failed.

The public was outraged by the actions of the expeditionary
force which had brazenly led Morrison into a death trap while
previously binding themselves to a truce which permitted his
freedom. The authorities said little, waiting for the passion to
blow over. In the meantime, men like Judge Dugas, who never
admitted perpetrating any wrongdoing in the case, were strongly
convinced that because Morrison was alleged to have killed a
man, no matter who, he would have to stand and answer for it.
The method of capture, in the scheme of things, was immaterial.

In the meantime, members of the Caledonian Society put
aside their anger and embarrassment over being duped and ral-
lied to the support of the cause sponsored by Graham, Nicholson, and McLeod. Sufficient funds were raised to procure the
services of the best criminal lawyers Canada had to offer for the
defense of Donald Morrison.

As the months went by, the furor over the illicit capture
waned and talk turned instead to Morrison's actual trial set for
the autumn assizes. It was hoped by many that at last Donald
Morrison would have some sort of justice.

13

"THE QUEEN *VS* MORRISON"

OCTOBER 1889

It was Tuesday, October 1, and Sherbrooke was a hive of activity. The preliminary hearing into the Morrison case had been held in the second week of August; the actual arraignment and subsequent trial would begin today. And it was word of the trial which brought the crowds. Since early morning the courtroom had been packed to capacity, and it had taken several rows of policemen linking arms to keep the throng from invading the very floor of the courtroom itself. Though many also lined the paths and courthouse steps to catch a glimpse of the outlaw, there were those whose interest stemmed from a desire to see some of the best lawyers in the country who were gathered here to represent both the defendant and the Crown. Close to $3,000 had been collected to aid Morrison's cause and acquire the services of such distinguished criminal lawyers as J. N. Greenshields, Q.C., of Winnipeg (the same Greenshields who unwittingly set off the "mineshaft search" for Morrison in Black Lake) and François Lemieux, of Quebec City, the future chief justice of the Supreme Court of Quebec. Both would be assisted by John Leonard of Sherbrooke, the lawyer brother of Hugh and James of Stornoway.

The prosecution was duly represented by Charles Fitzpatrick, the province's deputy attorney general and future Chief Justice of the Supreme Court of Canada, assisted by L. C. Belanger of Montreal and O. H. Desmarais of St. Hyacinthe. Obviously Premier Mercier and his cabinet considered this an important trial.

Particular interest centered around Greenshields, Lemieux, and Fitzpatrick. Five years previously they had served as the defense for Louis Riel, the Métis rebel leader who was subsequently hanged in Regina for treason in 1885 and his part in the uprising at Batoche, Saskatchewan, in that same year. Now Fitzpatrick found himself opposing his former colleagues in another trial which had caught the imagination of Canadians across the country.

Morrison would appear before Judge Edward Turle Brooks, a remote, laconic, and stern individual. He would be assisted by Judge Wurtele.

Peter Spanyaardt had arrived on the Monday afternoon and checked into the Sherbrooke House, directly across from the Canadian Pacific Railway Station. He then went immediately to the jail, only to be refused permission to visit Morrison. He had expected it. He then asked about the prisoner's welfare and and was told his hip still bothered him; he limped noticeably. Morrison had given the jail staff no trouble during his five-month stay.

Like everyone else in town, Spanyaardt arrived early Tuesday morning at the old courthouse on William Street and had to fight his way through the mobs outside. Only with difficulty did he reach the table reserved for the press. As he sat down, a reporter for the Montreal *Gazette*, whom he knew well, asked if he'd heard that the barn on the old Morrison farm had mysteriously burned to the ground last evening around eleven o'clock, some sort of salute or protest or whatever to the trial.

The arraignment began at 10:15. Donald Morrison arrived, chained and closely guarded, and was led to the prisoner's box. He looked wan and expressionless and was quite obviously in pain. The grand jury was empaneled, with Judge Brooks confining his remarks to the technicalities of their duties. He then turned to Morrison, reminding him of the charges against him and asking him how he pleaded:

1. Charged with the willful murder of Lucius Jack Warren on June 22, 1888. He pleaded "not guilty."

2. Charged with arson, in the burning of a stable belonging to Auguste Duquette, May 9, 1888. He pleaded "not guilty."

3. Charged with arson in the burning of the house belonging to Auguste Duquette, May 30, 1888. He pleaded "not guilty."

4. Charged with shooting at James McMahon and Pierre Leroyer on April 22, 1889. He pleaded "not guilty."

Morrison would be tried only on the first charge.

John Leonard, counsel for Morrison then rose, asking that the case be fixed for Friday, October 4. Fitzpatrick, the Crown prosecutor objected. The defense, he said, had had time enough to prepare itself. Greenshields, for the defense, got to his feet, saying in a case of such importance too much latitude could not be given the defense, and he glanced at the judges who were already conferring together. Brooks nodded and turned back to the court. The case, he said solemnly, was fixed for Wednesday, October 2, unless the defense could show any valid reason for postponement.

It had begun raining Wednesday morning by the time Peter Spanyaardt reached William Street and the long steps leading up to the courthouse. He pulled up the collar of his coat and made his way through the crowd which, he estimated, must be half the population of the town. He was soon to discover that the *other* half had managed to fill the inside corridor and the courtroom itself, leaving him no alternative once again but to use a little force as he pushed his way down to the press table located on the floor of the court.

It was 9:25 A.M. Wednesday, October 2. He eased himself onto the hard seat, then took out his notebook and handful of pencils, arranging them neatly before him. Thus prepared, he nodded at a fellow reporter who had ensconced himself at the other end of the table, then looked about him.

Spanyaardt was immediately struck by the fact that the spectators were dressed in their Sunday best, as though this were some highlight of the social session. Here too, among them were the mayors and councilors of local municipalities, dignitaries, and the upper strata of the community. Behind Spanyaardt and to his right he noticed R. D. Morkill, the provincial collector of internal revenue; his brother, James Morkill; and Reverend

Barnes of the town. Mayor Bryant of Sherbrooke was several rows back, as well as other faces he recognized—Dr. Graham, Murdo Beaton, Hugh and James Leonard, and a myriad of others representing the Megantic region. He could see Sophia Morrison, half-hidden by the crowd, who was accompanied by her daughters, Christie MacArthur and Katie Morrison. He had heard that old Murdo Morrison had hoped to come, but it seemed the expenses for traveling and staying in Sherbrooke were too much for the couple and it was decided Sophia would attend the trial, with him following later, should aid be forthcoming to defray the costs.

9:30 A.M.

Spanyaardt turned back in his seat. He had covered a few murder trials in his career, but each time was fascinated by the awesome solemnity of the courtroom. Even now the only sounds were muffled whispers punctuated with sporadic coughs.

This courtroom was smaller than most, measuring what he guessed was about fifty feet in width and forty feet in depth. Four large windows, which swept up to the high ceilings, were on either side, giving the room its only real touch of brightness, though this effect was somewhat nullified by the room's dulled cream-white walls and over-all mustiness. The courthouse had been built fifty years before.

The room was plainly furnished with stained wood benches and additional chairs, and other essential courtroom trappings. These included the familiar gilt-framed portrait of busty Queen Victoria who stared benignly down on the surroundings from her hook on the wall behind the judge's bench. This bench, elevated enough to ensure domination over the proceedings, was located along the back wall. Opposite was the spectators' gallery, with its railing dividing the public from the main floor of the courtroom. The paneled prisoner's dock, directly ahead, stood within arm's length of the first row of the public stands, with the defense table to its right, the prosecution to its left. The witness box was directly to the judge's left while further to the left, along the side wall was the solidly paneled jury box containing two rows of chairs. Immediately in front of the judge were the court clerks and sheriff, with the press shoved off to one side.

9:45 A.M.

Donald Morrison arrived through a door to the left of the judge's bench fifteen minutes early. He appeared clean-shaven and looked self-assured in a dark suit buttoned high at the neck but left open from there down. He wore a white shirt, stiff winged collar, tie, and handcuffs. Flanking him on either side was Constable Edward Summerville of the Quebec Provincial Police, who had been with the expeditionary force in the Eastern Townships, and one Sergeant Burns of the prison staff. Jailer Reed took up his solemn position behind this procession, with two more guards trailing.

A murmur swept through the crowd as the prisoner moved awkwardly to the dock, waited patiently as the handcuffs were removed, then pulled himself inside, followed by Summerville and Burns. Reed and the other two guards took up their positions nearby. No sooner was this procedure completed than the room became still.

A moment later the door to the right of the bench opened and the judges, Brooks and Wurtele, appeared, Brooks leading. The high-pitched voice of the crier brought the crowd to its feet. The judges took their places and began sorting through their documents. Brooks soon glanced up, letting his eyes roam about the room, seeing all was in order.

The presiding judge was an aristocratic man with a broad forehead and mustache which reached back to collide with a set of flaring sideburns just below the tips of his ears. His thin, fine-featured face, befitting a man of his eminence, was a perfect match for his narrow frame. The thinness of his neck was exaggerated by his habit of wearing collars several times too large. The over-all effect left observers with the general impression that His Honor was a delicate individual instead of the rather robust person he actually was.

As a judge of the Supreme Court of Quebec, Brooks was far from being one of the favorites among defending lawyers. He was astute, shrewd, and unpredictable. His court was his domain; no one, defense or prosecutor, ever forgot it. His decisions on cases in the past had left others with the feeling that he lacked the sensitivity needed for someone in his position. Appeals were not uncommonly made against his unpopular decisions or sentences.

Balancing Brooks on the other hand was Justice Wurtele, an intelligent, thoughtful person who showed a degree of compassion lacking in Brooks's make-up. Wurtele was both an adviser and interpreter to the senior judge.

10 A.M.

The proceedings opened with counsel for the defense Greenshields withdrawing his option for a mixed jury. His client was prepared to accept a jury entirely composed of English-speaking jurors, a request made two days before. Fitzpatrick for the Crown nodded his assent and Brooks granted the petition. The assembled witnesses were then removed from the court for the selection of the jury.

After much haggling and debate, which saw the defense reject fifteen prospective jurors, the Crown prosecution reject fourteen, the full complement of twelve was chosen: R. N. Turner, a farmer from North Hatley; William Warrick, farmer, Windsor Mills; Alfred Curtis, farmer, Stanstead; John Noyes, farmer, Barnston; Thomas Langmaid, farmer, Stanstead; Camille Millette, merchant, Richmond; James Mills, lumberman, Sherbrooke; John Horn, farmer, Barnston; Irwin Slack, farmer, Hatley; John Hurd, farmer, Barnston; Edgar Hawes, farmer, North Hatley and Henry Atkins, a farmer, Stanstead. The jury subsequently picked Camille Millette, the Richmond merchant as its foreman.

With the jury sworn, Belanger, for the Crown prosecution, rose from his chair and spoke directly to the jury saying the gallows was the penalty for Morrison's crime. "Thanks be to God," he said, not without emotion, "that the sensational stories published during the last year, holding Morrison up as the 'modern Rob Roy,' and all the stories invented by the newspapers about the case will now be set right. . . ." The case was simply one of murder; he continued, going on to relate the facts of Warren's death. But the defense objected. The Crown was arguing the case before the trial began, Lemieux said. The objection was overruled. Belanger concluded his opening remarks and called for his first witness, A. G. Woodward, coroner for the district of

St. Francis, who gave in evidence a summary of the inquest of June 1888 into the Duquette incident. He was followed by Dr. Millette, of Megantic, who explained the cause of Warren's death. Albert W. Pope, owner of the American House came next, telling how he had found the warrant for Morrison's capture in Warren's pocket after he was shot.

Greenshields' cross-examination of the witness brought an objection from the Crown when he asked if there was a general rumor about Warren "doing something else" as a living. Greenshields addressed himself to Brooks explaining the importance in establishing whether or not Lucius Warren had the reputation of being a dangerous man.

Justice Brooks: "You asked what was Warren's reputation? Surely you don't mean to establish that his business . . . was shooting people?"

Greenshields: "This is my question. Did this man Warren go about armed, threatening and shooting people?"

The objection was sustained.

Greenshields' expression remained unchanged. He again addressed Pope: "Did the deceased in your presence give expressions to an intention of shooting Morrison?"

Fitzpatrick was again on his feet. He objected that it had yet been established that Warren had made any hostile demonstration at the time of the shooting. The defense argued that the previous threat may have had a serious effect on the mind of the prisoner, playing an important role in the shooting.

Fitzpatrick countered: "In the event that no proof will be made that these threats caused Warren to make hostile demonstrations at the time of the shooting, the question whether he made previous threats cannot be considered now. It might create a wrong impression with the jury. Let my learned friend first prove Warren made a move to execute those threats."

Greenshields turned to the witness stand where Pope, somewhat confused, braced himself for the next question. Greenshields opened his mouth to speak, but Justice Brooks called a recess. It was noon.

Following lunch, the court resumed, with Greenshields recalling Albert Pope back to the witness stand, asking again if Warren had mentioned his intention of shooting Morrison. The witness replied he had heard the deceased "threaten the prisoner," but he was unaware that Warren carried a revolver. It was a matter of common knowledge, he explained, that Warren had a warrant for Morrison's arrest. Greenshields, leaning a hand on the witness box, nodded and stood back, indicating he would ask no more question of the witness for the present. Pope stepped down and went back to his seat, nodding pleasantly at Morrison, who returned a cautious smile.

The Crown then called George C. Mayo, the visiting collector of customs from the state of Maine, who stated under oath that at the time of the shooting he found Warren's body in the street. The warrant for Morrison's arrest was in Warren's pocket and his revolver was near the body. Not cross-examined by the defense, Mayo looked about him, then stepped down to make room for Thomas Beatty, a miller from Lowell, Maine, who also had witnessed the shooting. Belanger handed the revolver to the witness asking him to identify it. Beatty took it gingerly, then asked if it was supposed to be loaded.

Judge Brooks peered over the edge of the bench. Loaded? he asked. Surely not. Belanger stepped forward, taking the weapon from the Maine miller, saying that if it pleased the court he would have the gun removed from the room because indeed it was still loaded; his face showed a trace of embarrassment.

In the meantime, Beatty testified to hearing a shot and turning to see the deceased drop to the ground, though he was unable to see who fired the shot. When the weapon was returned to the courtroom unloaded, Beatty confirmed it as the revolver he'd seen beside Warren.

The Crown then called Joseph H. Morin to the witness stand. The justice of the peace from Sweetsburgh, Missisquoi County, he testified to issuing the warrant for Morrison's arrest on charges of arson and shooting with intent to kill. He told the court he had given it first to Bailiff Edwards, then to Lucius Warren, the American. The latter, Morin stated, was given the oath of allegiance to the Queen, then entrusted with the warrant. Cross-examined by Greenshields, Morin admitted he knew Warren was an alien. Who witnessed the procedure, he was asked? He paused for a moment, then said Jospeh Thibaudeau (a local notary) was the witness, who also acted as Morin's clerk. Greenshields asked him to speak up and he repeated his answer. The defense lawyer nodded, considered another question, but instead walked directly back to his desk, saying he would have no more questions at this time.

The afternoon of the first day of *The Queen* vs *Morrison* trial was almost over. Crown counsel Belanger looked at his watch, then decided to call one more witness, Donald Graham, a Megantic shopkeeper. After he was sworn, Belanger asked him to relate what he had seen of the shooting. Graham, obviously flustered, paused for a moment, then told the court in a voice that barely cleared a whisper how he saw Warren and Morrison come together and hear Morrison saying, "Keep clear." He said it twice, the witness told the court. Belanger told him to speak louder, then asked if Warren said anything in reply. Graham said he had, for he kept repeating, "Don't worry, don't worry." After this, Graham said he saw Morrison drawing his revolver. Graham stopped, asking for a glass of water.

The courtroom was hushed, every eye watching Graham swallow several mouthfuls from the water glass. Then he continued, saying he saw the deceased putting his hand to his hip but didn't have time to remove his gun before Morrison fired. He also witnessed Morrison walking away cool and unconcerned.

This testimony brought a stir from the spectators. It soon ended as Greenshields for the defense rose solemnly from the table and approached the stand. He asked the witness when he realized something was happening. Graham blinked, then said he knew there would be trouble when he saw the two men come together. Was the witness *sure* Warren never raised his pistol before Morrison fired? Yes, said Graham, he was certain. Greenshields nodded and glanced at Judge Brooks. He had no more questions, he said. Brooks nodded, conferred briefly with Justice Wurtele, then turned back to the courtroom, adjourning the case until the next day, Thursday, at ten o'clock.

Eustache Roy was Thursday morning's first witness. He took the stand boldly and told under oath how he and his brother Antoine had stepped from Antoine's blacksmith shop to see what was going on. He saw the shooting and watched Morrison step back. He related other details. When the Crown turned him over for cross-examintion, the defense said it wasn't necessary. Next came George Rodrigue, the farmer from Three Lakes.

Fitzpatrick crossed the floor and stopped before the witness, giving the man time to settle himself. He was then asked where he was at the time of the shooting. Rodrigue explained he was sitting on the veranda of the house next to Graham's shop, when he heard someone shout, "There is Morrison!" He looked up and saw Morrison stop when Warren had walked up to him. The "outlaw" spoke first, telling Warren to keep away. Morrison had also said, "Let me pass," several times. Fitzpatrick moved in closer to the witness, asking him how far apart the two men were. Rodrigue thought for a moment, then replied, "About fifteen feet." Fitzpatrick's eyebrows rose and fell. Tucking his thumbs into pockets in his vest, he walked slowly over to the jury, then wheeled about, and came back. And about the guns? he asked, letting his voice trail off. Rodrigue looked at the man before him, then glanced swiftly at the judges. Morrison, he said quietly, drew his revolver when he told Warren for the first time to keep away.

When Fitzpatrick had finished with his witness, François Lemieux stepped back from the defense table, nodded at the Crown prosecutors, then advanced within several feet of the witness stand. For a moment he said nothing, then asked almost casually if the witness had seen any document which Warren might have handed to Morrison. Rodrigue shook his head. "No," he said.

"You did not hear Warren say he had a warrant for him?"

Judge Brooks interrupted. "The witness stated already all he heard."

Rodrigue looked from Fitzpatrick to Brooks and back. "I did not hear him say anything of the kind," he snapped.

Lemieux seemed pleased. He leaned in closer to the witness. "Did not Morrison say, 'Don't fire or I shall fire too'?"

The farmer nooded. "That is what I understood.'"

Lemieux stepped back, rubbing his hands, asked a few less pertinent questions, then dismissed Rodrigue.

Antoine Roy, the Megantic blacksmith, was next. Asked by

Belanger what he had seen, Roy told the Crown prosecutor he saw that "Morrison had a cane in his hand at the time of the encounter and when Morrison jumped over the ditch the stick disappeared and he drew his firearm out of his pocket and pointed it toward Warren." Questioned by Lemieux moments later, he admitted seeing Morrison raise the revolver three times, then lower it three times. He saw that Warren also had a revolver in his hand, pointed at Morrison. Lemieux nodded, bringing his hands behind him. Who, he asked, had leveled his revolver at the other man first? Antoine Roy, confused glanced at the Crown prosecutors' table, then back at the lawyer before him. Morrison, he said slowly, shot Warren only *after* the latter had leveled the revolver at him.

A voice from behind the pair startled them both. Lemieux swung around to find that one of the jurors, who had been making copious notes, was asking if the conversation between Morrison and the deceased might be repeated. Antoine Roy looked at Judge Brooks, then said Morrison had used the word "revolver," to which Warren replied, "I have a warrant."

Lemieux was unflustered. "Is it possible he said 'I am Warren' instead of saying 'I have a warrant'?"

Antoine Roy nodded. "It is possible. I don't speak the English language very much."

Lemieux smiled. "Did you see any document in the hands of Warren?"

"No, sir."

"The only document in Warren's hand was a *revolver?*"

Roy's pause was filled with a comment from the bench. "A revolver is no document," Brooks snapped.

Lemieux smiled to himself. "Well, it is something," he said without looking at Brooks.

Antoine Roy, confused by it all, returned to the main issue by saying, "That is all Warren had in his hand." Lemieux thanked him and went back to the defense table, while Desmarais for the Crown asked for a re-examination. Judge Brooks nodded.

Turning back to the blacksmith Desmarais asked how much time had elapsed between the revolvers being removed from the two men's pockets. The witness paused briefly, answering that he thought about a minute and a half from the time Morrison had his revolver before Warren drew his and another minute after this Warren was shot.

At the press table Peter Spanyaardt pushed his legs out before him and stretched his arms. Fingers of his right hand were aching from making notes and his posterior was aching from sitting. From the look of the other reporters around him, they weren't any better off. Trying to catch every word and commit it to paper wasn't easy. As he looked up, he realized the next witness was already into his testimony.

Nelson Leet found the courtroom hot. He wiped a handkerchief quickly across his brow, trying at the same time to catch what Fitzpatrick was asking him. When he finished mopping, he asked the Crown prosecutor to repeat his question. Fitzpatrick said he only wanted the hotel owner to tell the court what he had seen during the shooting. Leet agreed and without any trace of nervousness told how Warren had come up beside his chair on the veranda and asked if the man walking down the street was Morrison. He then went on to tell exactly what happened, ignoring Fitzpatrick halfway through his testimony when the prosecutor shuffled his feet and looked somewhat agitated.

When the witness was finished, Fitzpatrick shook his head and asked in a loud voice why Leet's testimony before the court varied with the deposition he had given following the shooting. Leet, nonplused, admitted he had not said all he knew at the time. Fitzpatrick grunted and walked back to the table, returning with the original deposition, of which he read a portion aloud to the court.

Greenshields objected. "In fairness to the witness, Your Honor, I would ask that the whole deposition be read, and not only part of it. The balance of the deposition would confirm the witness' statements . . . perfectly."

Fitzpatrick was visibly annoyed. He swung around to face Greenshields. "Oh my honored friend, we shall settle that soon. I shall have an application to make after recess." He then turned to the judge who agreed it was lunchtime.

When the trial resumed at two o'clock, the only person missing was Nelson Leet. With everyone assembled, the courthouse echoed to the shouts of Leet's name. Finally Judge Brooks leaned over to Justice Wurtele; they exchanged whispers. Brooks then sent the bailiff in search of the errant hotel keeper and at 2:15 Nelson Leet strode alone into the courtroom at the precise moment legal action was proceeding against him.

Fitzpatrick wasn't amused. He asked his witness, "Who did you speak to during the recess?"

Leet settled himself comfortably in the witness box before replying, "To Mr. Malcolm Matheson and another witness in the case, but I said nothing about my evidence which I still have to give."

The Crown prosecutor looked wearily at the bench. Brooks yawned, indicating with the nod for Fitzpatrick to carry on. Turning to the deposition, reading a section dealing with Warren having trouble taking the revolver from his pocket, finally managing to level it at Morrison. Morrison, the deposition stated, only drew his revolver when Warren had his out, though Leet wasn't sure who had leveled the revolver at his opponent first. Morrison did fire his.

Fitzpatrick glanced up at his witness, asking him if this were true or not true.

"Not true," was the reply, and for the first time the courtroom came alive. While order was restored, the Crown prosecutor had walked slowly across the floor and stood thoughtfully before the jury, waiting for silence. Only then did he speak.

"What portion of your evidence isn't true?" he asked, facing the jurors.

Defense immediately objected. When the witness said the deposition wasn't true, he meant his evidence hadn't been taken down correctly.

Fitzpatrick listened, then turned to the judge, while remaining before the jury. He requested that the witness be excluded from the court until the argument was settled. Judge Brooks agreed. Leet was escorted into the hall and the doors closed behind him. He remained there, under guard.

The matter wasn't settled and Nelson Leet was returned to the witness stand to indicate which portions of his deposition weren't true. The portion about the revolver, he said, wasn't quite true. What he meant at the time was he saw Warren draw his gun out first. Fitzpatrick once again referred to the deposition which, he said, stated that he, Leet, saw Morrison draw his revolver. Leet shook his head. He hadn't said that during his testimony for the deposition. Fitzpatrick moved back across the room and was about to speak when defense lawyer Greenshields interrupted him. Fitzpatrick, paying no attention to his learned friend, approached the bench, asking that interruptions by the counsel for the defense should be stopped.

Greenshields moved out from behind the table and strode into the middle of the courtroom, remonstrating with the Crown prosecutors. "If the *learned* counsel on the other side were more attentive to what the witness said than what counsel says amongst themselves, he would not have so much difficulty."

An audible sigh from the bench silenced them both. "I ask it as a personal favor," Judge Brooks said curtly, "that cross-talk between counsels not take place." The counsels agreed.

Fifteen minutes later Greenshields was cross-examining the witness: ". . . you told us all that Morrison did, Mr. Leet, now tell us, what did Warren do? Did Warren drink anything before he met Morrison that day?"

Leet nodded. The deceased, he said, had about five glasses of beer. As for Warren's reaction when facing Morrison, the hotel owner said he saw the barrel of Warren's gun first, then saw both barrels leveled. Warren's hand was on his revolver in his pocket and was partly out before Morrison drew. He waited then for Greenshields' next question.

"If Morrison had not shot first, would not Warren have shot Morrison if he could hit him?"

It was Belanger's turn to get to his feet. He objected to the question. The objection was sustained.

Greenshields took a new tack. Could the witness see if Warren's revolver was cocked, he said, handing the revolver first to Leet, then to the jury, to verify it was a self-cocking weapon which would not need cocking before pulling the trigger. The question to Leet was left unanswered and the hotel owner was asked to step down.

The Crown turned to its next witness, A. W. Gough, a builder from Boston who witnessed the shooting, though his testimony shed no new light on the case. No sooner had Lemieux wound up his short cross-examination than Charles Fitzpatrick announced to a surprised court that it would be calling no more of the witnesses it had subpoenaed, which included two young women who had seen some of what took place from a balcony directly above the spot where the shooting took place.

At the press table all the heads were down as the reporters wrote furiously. Peter Spanyaardt glanced up long enough to see the surprised looks upon the faces of the defense counsels, Greenshields, Lemieux, and Leonard. Behind him the courtroom had broken into unrestrained whispers, and as he wrote a new lead for his story, he heard Judge Brooks adjourn proceedings until Saturday morning, at ten o'clock.

Spanyaardt's story for the Saturday edition of the *Star*, found under the leadline WARREN'S THREATS AGAINST MORRISON, covered almost three columns. It began:

> SHERBROOKE, October 5—The defence for Morrison are smiling today. They are hopeful and think that the fact that the prosecution [are] only using part of the witnesses subpoenaed argues well. It seems that the Crown has been somewhat disappointed in the men they have summoned to testify and it is stated by some of them that they had been locked up in a room and underwent a severe examination as to what they could testify.
>
> The defence was busily engaged last night arranging their evidence. . . .

Saturday, October 5, 1889. The weather hadn't been good all week. Today was no exception. Well before the trial resumed Spanyaardt slipped over to the prosecution, asking Charles Fitzpatrick for some comment on the proceedings. Fitzpatrick wasn't eager to say anything, but commented that he thought the Crown was "sure of at least a verdict of manslaughter," while Morrison's lawyers "express confidence in a verdict of acquittal."

When Donald Morrison arrived in court fifteen minutes before ten o'clock, he appeared to be more like his old self. Though

still limping noticeably, he held his head high, nodding to familiar faces in the crowd as he crossed the courtroom to stop before
the prisoner's dock while Summerville removed his handcuffs.

The judges, Brooks and Wurtele, took their places exactly on
the hour. Belanger, for the Crown, opened proceedings by asking
permission to recall Justice of the Peace Joseph Morin.

Defense objected. Lemieux argued that the prosecution had
rested its case yesterday and had no right to change its mind this
morning. It should not be permitted to bring on more witnesses.
Belanger, ignoring him, asked for special application to recall
Morin.

While the defense fumed, Brooks and Wurtele conferred together, then gave Belanger permission to proceed. With Morin
installed in the witness box, Belanger asked him, "Did Lucius
Warren have any questions upon being sworn in . . . ?" Morin
nodded. Warren had asked if, being made special constable, he
had the right to carry a revolver.

Greenshields was on his feet. Objection, he shouted, the law
explains the duties and the rights of a constable and the instructions by the justice of the peace. The objection was overruled.

Morin continued. He had told Warren that he might continue
to carry a revolver, but to be careful not to use it other than in
self-defense. Belanger acknowledged the answer, then asked
what steps Bailiff Edwards had taken to arrest Morrison previous
to the issuance of the warrant to Warren? Defense didn't like the
question. Edwards, it argued, was the best witness to answer the
question and he hadn't been called. Objection was sustained, and
the defense called its first witness.

Malcolm Matheson came forward, took the oath, and sat
down in the witness box. Greenshields, standing before him,
asked him first how long he had known the accused and was told
for eleven years. The defense lawyer then waited a moment or
two, letting the jury study the new witness, then asked him what
had been the general character of the accused, regarding, say,
his peacefulness.

It was now the prosecution's turn to raise objections, saying
everyone was supposed to have a good character for "peacefulness" until the contrary was proved. Greenshields smiled,
knowing Belanger was aware that the defense was attempting to

force him into a position where the Crown would have to *prove* that Morrison was a lawless character to begin with.

Judge Brooks, also aware of this, overruled the objection, noting that the jury knew nothing of the accused and neither did the court. It would therefore be of great value, he said, to have the prisoner's character established. Greenshields turned back to his witness. What then, he asked, was Morrison's reputation?

"He was highly esteemed and respected in the vicinity," Matheson said quietly. Asked if the witness knew Warren, he replied yes, Warren had been in his store the Monday before the shooting, asking if he knew of Morrison's whereabouts. Matheson had answered that he did not. Greenshields then asked if Warren had said anything further. Matheson nodded. Warren had said, "I will have his Christly soul either dead or alive." A murmur swept through the courtroom, bringing Judge Brooks's head up, but he said nothing.

"Was it generally known," Greenshields asked the witness, "that Warren had made threats against Morrison?"

Objection.

Greenshields shrugged and turned to the bench. "In the beginning of the trial," he said slowly, "it was established by the Crown that public rumor knew that Warren had a warrant against Morrison. Now the defense, Your Honor, has the right to show that it was equally known by the public and must have been known to Morrison, that Warren had threatened to bring him in alive *or* dead." Greenshields stopped, letting his eyes now run along the two rows of jurymen, before continuing: "If Warren, the supposed constable, and we shall prove later that he *was* no constable at all, could attempt an arrest on the strength of the rumor that must have been known to Morrison, then Morrison was in a similar position as to the rumor that Warren wanted him dead or alive."

Fitzpatrick jumped to his feet. "The court has already given the accused the extremest latitude by admitting evidence of threats made by Warren and probably the court did well in giving him *all* the latitude, but I object to a proof that the threats justified the shooting."

Judge Brooks looked puzzled. He leaned over to have a whispered conversation with Wurtele, then sat back again. The objection would be sustained, he said, because at this stage of the case he could not allow such evidence. However, should it be proved that Warren *did* make threats and that these were carried to Morrison, then the prisoner would receive full benefit of the evidence. Greenshields acknowledged the remark and told Matheson to step down, the Crown waving its right to cross-examination.

John McLeod of Whitton took Matheson's place in the witness box. He was asked about a meeting with Warren two days before the shooting. McLeod then told the court that Warren had said should he get his eye on Donald Morrison, he would go no further.

"Who would go no further?"

McLeod looked at Greenshields, momentarily confused, then added, "Donald Morrison. Warren repeated it twice. The second time he said, 'I just want to get my eye on him and he won't go any further.'"

Greenshields: "Had you previously heard Warren make threats to shoot Morrison and what did you understand when Warren said Morrison would go no further?"

Objection.

Overruled.

McLeod: "I understood Warren to mean that he would shoot Morrison."

Greenshields then asked about the meeting when McLeod knew this impression was conveyed to Morrison. But Belanger objected a second time. Greenshields argued that it was admissible to bring Warren's threats "home." Objection was overruled. McLeod told how he was present when his wife told Morrison there was a man "at the lake who will put a bullet through you." Greenshields asked what "the lake" meant, and McLeod said it referred to Megantic. Stepping up close to the witness box, the defense lawyer then said: "Now under your oath, have you any doubt that Morrison thought she referred to anyone else except Warren?"

"I have not the slightest doubt that Morrison knew that no one else but Warren was referred to," he said without hesitation.

The crowded courtroom, holding its breath for the answer, suddenly sighed. Feet shuffled, chairs scraped, and Greenshields thanked the witness, then stepped aside for the Crown's cross-examination.

Charles Fitzpatrick came across from the prosecution table and asked the witness immediately if he had actually told Morrison about the warrant against him. McLeod shook his head. Judge Brooks told the witness to speak up. "No," he said. He did not see Morrison from the moment Warren spoke to him until the shooting, not knowing where Morrison was at the time.

"It is rather strange that you did not know where he lived, is it not?"

"I did not know whether Morrison had any home . . . when he was driven off his farm."

Fitzpatrick jammed his thumbs into his vest. "Did you ever see him within a month previous to the shooting?"

"I cannot say I did, excepting that one time at McLean's."

"How do you explain that you, knowing Donald since his earliest youth, never told him of the warrant?"

Objection. The Crown was embarrassing the witness uselessly and *assuming* that the witness saw Morrison and would not tell him.

Objection overruled.

McLeod eyed Fitzpatrick. "I did not see Morrison."

Fitzpatrick: "You remember that ten days before the shooting Warren said something which you took to be threats against Morrison. Did you tell anyone of these threats?"

McLeod flushed. "I made it public. I told Angus Smith. I let it be known generally."

Judge Brooks leaned forward, looking not unkindly on the witness. "Did you call a public meeting and announce the fact?"

"No, I told people I met."

"That is not making it public," said the judge edgily, then looked at the prosecution. Fitzpatrick had no further questions.

A. N. Paton was the third witness for the defense to take the stand. He had boarded at the American House when Warren was staying there and he was asked what sort of conversation he had with the deceased prior to the shooting. Paton was nervous. He clutched the railing of the witness box, stammering that he had once asked Warren, "Have you got any word about Morrison?" Warren, he said, had replied, "Not yet." To this Paton had said that Morrison was a pretty smart fellow. Warren answered that he did not care and that if he got a sight of Morrison he would "fix him."

Greenshields: "What did you understand him to mean by the words 'fix him'?"

Paton: "I understood that he was going to shoot him. That's how I understood him."

Had Warren pushed the issue any further? "Yes," said the witness, "Warren carried a revolver on his hip and flaunted it around pretty freely."

Paton faced a short cross-examination, then was dismissed. Other witnesses were called before Judge Brooks announced a forty-five-minute recess.

Peter Spanyaardt was glad of it. He stood and stretched, watching the jury file out of the courtroom. I would give anything to know what was going on in their minds, he thought, as he stepped around the table, moved past the other reporters, and walked casually over to the prisoner's box. Donald Morrison was leaning against the rail, and Spanyaardt asked how he thought the proceedings were going. Morrison's face brightened. "Things are going well," he said. "I feel first rate." Though the guards, including Constable Summerville and Jailer Reed eyed them both, no one moved to interrupt them. They talked for a moment or two, then Spanyaardt wished him good luck and was heading toward his seat when he noticed two women sitting directly behind the prisoner's dock. Though neither looked familiar, the prettier of the two seemed somehow important to the surroundings. With only minutes left before the judges would return, the reporter slipped quietly over to defense lawyer John Leonard and, leaning down close, asked who the two women were. Leonard glanced casually back, caught a smile, and returned it. They were friends of Morrison's, he said, both from Spring Hill. On the right was Augusta McIver. He was naming the second when the clerk announced the court was back in session. As the reporter reached his seat, he had made up his mind that a talk with Augusta was important.

The trial resumed, with the defense calling Norman McDonald. Though he appeared calm, Spanyaardt could see his eyes darting about the courtroom before settling on Greenshields' comforting smile. He was to tell the court what he had seen of the shooting.

McDonald's voice, whether he realized it or not, came in a whisper. Judge Brooks told him to speak up. McDonald nodded and continued, saying he had come out of Malcolm Matheson's store at the same moment Donald Morrison was telling Warren to stand back. "I looked in the direction of the voice and saw Warren with his revolver pointed at Morrison. The latter took a quick step back and fired." McDonald stopped, looked around, feeling better, then continued without being prodded. "A very short time elapsed between the time I saw Warren with the revolver in his hand and the shot. It was just one instant. I did not see Morrison's revolver until he stepped back. . . ." He stopped a second time. Greenshields nodded and he went on, "I . . . went to the body, then turned back. I only went to the hotel when I was called back in my capacity as undertaker. . . ."

The tension building up during his account suddenly snapped as chuckles and outright laughter broke like a dam from the crowded courtroom. Brooks reached for his gavel to restore order, thought better of it, and waited as the defense stepped aside for the Crown's cross-examination. Asked how he had seen the actual shooting, McDonald answered, "Warren stood with his right side to me and Morrison stood in front of him." In trying to make his explanation clearer, and not succeeding, Fitzpatrick suggested he might demonstrate.

With the court's approval McDonald stepped down, placing Fitzpatrick first in Morrison's position, then changed his mind and placed him where Warren would have stood. Spanyaardt saw with amusement that Fitzpatrick was not all that co-operative, for he kept turning his back on the witness when placed in either of the two positions. Finally McDonald managed to show where he stood in relation to Warren and Morrison. Fitzpatrick had no more questions.

Next the defense called Charles Braddock of Megantic to the stand. He told the court he knew little of the prisoner, but was well acquainted with the deceased, who he said was from Charleston, Maine. He had several conversations with Warren on the veranda of the American House and quoted himself as saying to Warren, "You have not got Morrison." Warren had replied, "I will get him." Braddock then said, "You had better let that job go," to which Warren answered, "I can shoot as fast as he can."

Greenshields: "What was his profession?"

Braddock: "Warren was a professional whiskey smuggler."

Greenshields: "Do you know if this man was a dangerous man?"

Fitzpatrick came quickly around the table, objecting furiously. The question, he said was irrelevant.

Greenshields swung back toward the prosecution. "After proving the threats by Warren," he snapped, "I am entitled to prove that he was a man likely to carry out threats." The objection was overruled. The defense waited for the witness's answer: "I did not know Warren to be a violent or dangerous man."

After several more witnesses gave their testimony, Greenshields asked the farmer François Thivierge to come forward. Speaking in French, he told how he had witnessed the shooting from the veranda of Leet's hotel. He testified how he was sure Warren was the first to draw his revolver. Morrison drew his gun afterward, telling Warren to keep back.

Under cross-examination, Thivierge said he knew Warren only by sight, not by name. Others too had given their testimony with Justice Wurtele translating it into English for Judge Brooks. The farmer continued, recalling how he saw Morrison with a cane in his right hand which he changed to his left, then drew his revolver first, to cover Warren. At this point, Thivierge said he didn't like what he saw, so he headed inside when the shot was fired. Belanger shook his head, noting aloud that the witness had contradicted himself, saying Warren drew his gun first, then saying Morrison had. Judge Wurtele explained this to the jury.

With Thivierge's cross-examination complete, Greenshields came around toward the bench, saying the defense would rest its case. Behind him, Charles Fitzpatrick was pleased. He too approached the bench, asking that the judge's charge to the jury and addresses of both Crown and defense be postponed until Monday. Judge Brooks stroked his long, fluffy sideburns, thought for a moment, then announced that court was adjourned till Monday morning.

The courtroom broke into chaos. Spanyaardt moved quickly

to intercept the Crown prosecutors, but the guards about Donald Morrison held him back as the accused was led past. Spanyaardt cursed his luck, then turned to the two women behind the prisoner's docket. They too were lost in the crowd.

Sunday, October 6. With a free day on his hands Peter Spanyaardt had time to write the recent events of the trial and track down a few facts which had been on his mind. He had mentioned Augusta McIver in his news report referring to the "pretty girl whom the police have allowed to remain right in the rear of the dock and who hovers over Morrison like a guardian angel." He hoped to interview her over the weekend only to learn she had returned to her parents' home in Spring Hill and wasn't expected back in Sherbrooke until Monday. Spanyaardt considered and rejected the idea of taking himself out to Spring Hill. It was too far, and besides, he had enough to occupy his mind. Also this evening he had promised Sidney Broderick dinner, on expenses. He was looking forward to a frank discussion of the trial and its possible outcome.

During drinks at the bar of the Sherbrooke House their conversation centered particularly around Donald Morrison, with Spanyaardt speculating, on rather flimsy evidence, on an acquittal. The lawyer grunted merrily, saying he hoped his friend hadn't put his money where his decision was. Why an acquittal? Spanyaardt leaned forward over the low table. The Crown had run out of steam. It hadn't called on its full complement of witnesses and the defense got more out of them on cross-examination than the Crown did. Broderick sipped slowly at his Scotch and sat back comfortably. Had Peter considered the possibility that the Crown might not have called all its witnesses because it felt the case won? Spanyaardt laughed out loud. The Crown, he retorted, had rested its case before *more* damage was done.

Broderick's face broke into a grin. Spanyaardt's decision was too hasty, he said, apart from being too obvious. Law had never been based on the obvious. As they walked to the dining room, the lawyer advised his friend that one important aspect would influence the trial over the next few days: the defense's address to the jury. It held the key. The defense must forcibly challenge the legality of Warren as constable. The jury would have to be thoroughly convinced that Warren had *no legal right* to arrest Morrison, and if they were not convinced, Spanyaardt's theory of acquittal would go out the window.

For dessert, Spanyaardt ordered maple-sugar pie, which Broderick eyed but refused, saying his waistline couldn't afford it. The temptation was too great, however, and as he sliced off the first mouthful, he glanced at his friend, saying there was another important aspect of the trial which was worth considering. Judge Brooks was an unknown factor, and from past trials over which he had presided, His Honor's addresses to the jury had from time to time been construed as . . . well . . . Broderick stopped to look down at the pie on his plate. Without finishing his sentence he lifted the fork and began eating.

From his seat in the courtroom Monday morning, October 7, Peter Spanyaardt watched the seats fill with the prominent citizens of Sherbrooke and surrounding communities, still faithfully arriving in their best clothes as they had done throughout the trial. The only dreary lot appeared on the stroke of ten o'clock. They were the members of the jury whose confinement since the previous Wednesday had left them looking somewhat sullen and unkempt as they filed into the jury box.

Donald Morrison had taken his place without undue notice while the courtroom hummed with whispered conversations and greetings. Augusta McIver was back in her place, along with the same friend. She and Donald managed a few brief words before the clerk announced the arrival of Judges Brooks and Wurtele.

Spanyaardt had learned earlier that John Leonard and J. N. Greenshields would address the jury on behalf of the defense, with François Lemieux giving the opening remarks. Charles Fitzpatrick and L. C. Belanger would speak for the Crown.

The courtroom had not yet settled down, and Brooks himself was messing about with papers on his desk, when Spanyaardt, glancing idly across the room, caught Belanger's attention. For a moment their eyes held fast, then without expression Belanger looked away. It was a small incident, but nevertheless made Spanyaardt smile to himself.

It seemed that Belanger, following adjournment of the trial

on Saturday, had become disenchanted with the press and its reporting of the trial. He had threatened to have the court exclude the newspapermen from this day's proceedings. The ruse hadn't worked, and Spanyaardt noticed that Belanger was still fuming, possibly also because John Leonard and the defense had stated unequivocally that should the Crown try such a tactic, it would be "strenuously opposed by the defense." Spanyaardt was still chuckling over this morning's brief eye-to-eye encounter when the court was called to order. The defense would begin.

François Lemieux stepped before the jury, his eyes glinting with explosive zeal. He was known for his fiery clashes with Crown prosecutions on many occasions, and he spoke English with a flair which put much extra meaning into that language. But today he spoke in French. Quietly he told members of the jury that they should consider the "following points of law." First, Warren was not a British subject, therefore he could not be appointed to the charge of special constable: it was not *possible*. Secondly, his nomination being thus null and void, Warren could not arrest the accused under any circumstances. Lemieux paused, waiting to have the attention of each juror before saying that, thirdly, Warren could not be an "assistant" to Bailiff Edwards, which brought home the fourth point: the document given Warren was *null and void*, leaving him no authority to carry out what he had planned. Finally, if the defense's propositions are reasonable and true and applicable to the facts, if Lucius Warren acted in such a manner that the prisoner would have been justified in thinking his life was in danger, his shooting of Warren *was in self-defense*.

Lemieux, pacing back and forth, now stood motionless before the jury, his arms folded, legs slightly apart. He remained thus for several seconds before saying that under the Consolidated Statutes of Quebec, Warren had to be *appointed* by *two* justices of the peace. He had been only *sworn in*, not appointed, by *one*, Joseph H. Morin. Mr. Morin was also bound to transmit a notice of same to the secretary of the province, under Section 3 of the Consolidated Statutes of Canada. He had failed to do so. The warrant was originally addressed to Edwards, in accordance with Canadian law, Lemieux explained, it must be addressed either to a justice of the peace or a constable, and Edwards was

neither. Further, Edwards did not, according to the law-co-
operate with his pretended assistant Warren, either directly or
indirectly, as he ought to have done. The warrant also did not al-
lege that the prisoner had committed a crime, but rather he was
only *suspected* of having done so. Besides, the lawyer said
grimly, the warrant should possess all the requirements of an indictment, which it hadn't.

Across the room Peter Spanyaardt recalled Broderick's words.
They proved correct. But why would Lemieux address the court
in *French* when much of it, if not all, would be lost on the jurors,
many of whom spoke *only* English. If he had his reasons,
Spanyaardt discovered later, he was sharing them with no one.

Charles Fitzpatrick for the Crown now stood before the
court, countering at once the remarks of the defense. It would be
impossible to imagine, he said, that an alien who saw a felony
committed should stand by and let the thing be done, simply because he was an alien. Then turning dramatically to the jury, he
exclaimed, "Every man has the right to arrest a felon, alien or no
alien."

The remark brought François Lemieux angrily to his feet.
Pleading with the judges, he said Warren was not an eyewitness
to any felony, as his honorable friend had intimated, and . . .
Judge Brooks cut him short. Lemieux took his seat and listened
icily through the Crown's concluding remarks.

Defense then rose to ask if two of its members might give
the defense's closing address to the jury. Brooks conferred with
Wurtele. The permission was granted and John Leonard stood
before the twelve jurymen.

"It is with great diffidence for my own ability that I address
you," he said quietly, "because more able, more aged men should
occupy my position in the defense of the prisoner, but at the
same time I feel that if no other man in the court should raise
his voice in his defense, I ought." Leonard paused for a moment,
seeking the words which would convey his feelings.

"I was, as it were, brought up with Donald Morrison. I know
what he was, how he lived, and I know his excellent reputation,
against which no man that appeared in the witness box would
say a thing." As he talked, Leonard walked to the other side of
the jury box and now came back slowly, his voice loud and

steady. "Was it not natural that Morrison, when he met Lucius Warren drawing a revolver from his pocket . . . should have said to himself, 'There is the man who would murder me'?"

The young lawyer then went down through the list of witnesses, emphasizing what they had seen; Leet saw Warren leaving the hotel, going to meet Morrison, "the first revolver drawn, he says, was that of Warren." Leonard stopped, clearing a throat choked with emotion, then went on, "It was natural for Leet to follow Warren step by step and nobody could know the circumstances better and his evidence must be conclusive on this point. The Crown in vain tried to break him down in cross-examination, but I don't think there is any doubt in your mind that Lucius J. Warren, after all the threats he made, crossed the street with the sole intention of shooting Morrison." He then waved a hand airily back at the Crown's table and continued: "The prosecutor will try to impress upon your mind that Warren was a peace officer, but the first thing that precious peace officer did on that day was to break the peace by drawing his revolver. And in reviewing the case before you, I think you cannot feel that Morrison is guilty of cold, calculated, deliberate murder." He sat down.

Greenshields, rising for the defense, was less subtle. "It was for the same reason that we would crush the rattlesnake that crossed our path or kill the tiger in the Indian jungle without waiting for his final spring," he all but shouted as he faced the jury, that Warren died. Without pausing, he launched himself verbally at the prosecution, asking why the prisoner was so heavily guarded in court, "if not to impress the jury with the idea the prisoner was a most dangerous character?"

Greenshields paused and went on: "And in regard to the shooting of Warren by Morrison, you have now heard how Warren used to go around showing people his revolver, telling them that the weapon would stop Morrison, and if he could not arrest him, the pistol would. All these rumors were spread abroad and, two weeks before the shooting, Mrs. McLeod warned Morrison that there was a man at the lake who would put a bullet through him. . . ."

Greenshields had come within a stride of the jury. Now he stepped forward placing his broad hands along the top of the railing, his eyes settling on each juryman in turn. Finally, with his voice lowered so the words hardly reached the rest of the courtroom, he said, "Remember, gentlemen of the jury, that amongst all the witnesses which the Crown has brought forward there was not a single one who could prove that Morrison had ever made a threat whatever against Warren. And why did Warren not follow the common use of the law? He crossed the street, and as he meets Morrison he draws his revolver and tells him to go no further. Why did he do this?" Again Greenshields left the sentence punctuated with silence. Then, "simply because he thought there was more glory in taking this man a bleeding corpse than to take him alive. It would have been easy for him to say that he was an officer of the law and that he had an order to arrest him; that he did not intend to do violence, but that if he would not surrender he would call for assistance. . . ."

Greenshields continued for a moment, caught up in the utter stillness of the courtroom. Finally, he turned his full attention back to the jury, saying, "And can you put your hands on your hearts and say that the prisoner at the bar, when the shooting occurred, was not aware that his life was in danger?"

The crowd behind was hushed as Greenshields stepped back from the jury box and began again to describe each scene, each vignette, each moment, as he recounted the evidence from the movements of the witnesses before the shooting to the very second when Warren hit the ground, dead. Before he wound up the case for the defense he reminded the jury of the "compromise" verdict "because the jury might say, this man should receive some punishment though he does not merit the punishment asked for by the Crown."

Greenshields continued: "If the prisoner acted according as the testimony appears to you in self-defense, there should be no verdict of murder, nor one of manslaughter. If the Crown wishes to punish him, they can do so by trying him on the many other indictments they have brought against him. You have only to deal today with the charge of murder. To find him guilty of manslaughter you must show that he had no right to defend himself. I . . . trust you are not prepared to send this man to prison for life on the evidence adduced. Brave men . . . do not commit murder. It is committed for gain, for hatred, but not under the circumstances as those of which we know so well at this present time. The prisoner belongs to a fearless people, the Scots, men who believe that when they have rights, they are ready to fight for the preservation of these rights till their last drop of blood." The lawyer broke off, taking a handkerchief from his pocket to wipe his brow. At last he said he had taken more time than he should, "but I cannot help feeling the great and terrible responsibility that rests on *me*." Without another word, he walked deliberately back to his table and sat down.

If Greenshields final remarks to the jury were dynamically forceful for the defense, Charles Fitzpatrick for the Crown matched him sentence for sentence. It was obvious from the way he stepped up to the jury that he was in no mood for appeasement.

Planting himself firmly before the jurymen, he shot a finger out toward the prisoner's dock and barked, "We have a right to say to him, 'Cain, what hath thou done to thy brother Abel?'"

The courtroom was caught off guard. The jury, too, jerked back in their seats, as the Crown prosecutor stampeded through a detailed account of why a plea of self-defense had no significance in this case. Then he turned his ire on the defense, rebuking them for "scraping away the earth from the grave of Warren" in order to blacken his character. While hardly drawing breath, Fitzpatrick launched into a review of the evidence given over the past four days of the trial, re-examining the weaknesses of the defense's case, upholding the merits of the Crown's case, and finally he swung about to face the jury with such suddenness that several chairs scraped backwards out of his way. If their verdict was "not guilty," he snapped, "it would mean that any man could shoot an officer." Just as suddenly, his storm of words subsided and he spoke softly, telling the jury, it was theirs to decide between the fate of a human being and the demands of justice. He spoke on.

It was almost 4:30 in the afternoon when Crown prosecutor Belanger approached the jury. He at once refuted the legal objections raised earlier by the defense's François Lemieux. Greenshields was on his feet, demanding that the time for such an argument had passed. Justice Brooks overruled his objection, and Belanger repudiated the charge that the Crown was conducting the case based on the principle of blood for blood, an allegation made by the defense. He would have continued past five o'clock had not Justice Brooks interrupted, saying he saw no end to the wrangling. Fitzpatrick conferred with his fellow prosecutors, then approached the bench, saying they would let their charge to the jury rest. Brooks was pleased. Tomorrow morning he would address the court. At ten.

14

VERDICT

OCTOBER 1889

A strange stillness gripped the courtroom the next morning. It was Tuesday, October 8. On previous mornings, murmurs of conversation mingling with the shuffling of chairs and feet brought an added dimension of reality to the surroundings. The utter silence this day gave one the unnerving sensation that nothing was real; each person seemed to be taking part in a fantasy which would soon end with the coming down of the curtain and the sounds of applause.

The first glimpse of the handcuffed Morrison shuffling between the five armed guards broke the spell; it did not break the stillness.

Peter Spanyaardt had arrived well before eight o'clock. The crowds had already assembled outside the courthouse and moved restlessly about the spacious lawns or sat below the concrete pillars which flanked the front of the building. Apart from clearing up a few details (he'd been queried by his newspaper concerning certain court procedures), he hoped to find a few moments with Augusta McIver. He had seen her from a distance yesterday and had planned to corner her during the noon recess. But that had been cut short, in the hope that the addresses to the jury would be completed early. Following the adjournment last night, Judge Brooks expressed his annoyance that no time was left for him to charge the jury.

In the confusion which followed Monday's adjournment, Spanyaardt had missed Augusta again, though he had to admit her exits were hasty. No newspaperman had been lucky enough to talk with her. He had found that his eyes kept drifting in her direction most of the day on Monday, for she was a beautiful, dark-haired woman of smallish stature. Her change of expressions, matching the minor triumphs and moments of despair during the trial, fascinated him. He noted that her back seldom, if ever, touched the back of the bench. She sat erect, the only movement coming from her eyes, which darted tirelessly from the defense, to the Crown, to the bench, and inevitably back to Donald Morrison.

Today, Tuesday, she hadn't appeared. Spanyaardt was disappointed. At ten o'clock, with the arrival of the judges, the court rose. When the journalist glanced at the prisoner's box, he was surprised to see Augusta in her usual place, wearing a plain dress, her coat still over her shoulders; frustrated, Spanyaardt swore quietly to himself.

Morrison's friends, scattered throughout the courtroom, were full of apprehension. Yesterday they had praised Greenshields' eloquent address for the defense and had to stifle applause during Leonard's touching appeal to the jury. Fitzpatrick's address for the Crown had been as thunderous and deliberate as these friends were told it would be. But mostly, everyone feared what Justice Brooks would say this morning, for he was an unpredictable man. The judge wasted little time in opening his charge to the jury.

"Gentlemen of the jury," he began, looking up from the sheaf of handwritten pages resting before him, "the prisoner at the bar stands accused of one of the most serious offenses known. A homicide has been committed and we have gathered here for the past six days to decide whether the prisoner is guilty or not. I will detail in short the circumstances of the case." The judge, caught in mid-breath by a sudden dryness of the throat, took a sip from his water glass, then continued: "One of the counsels has said that you are to be guided by your own understanding, not by the court. That is what I have always held. I have not the slightest wish to interfere with the right of the jury. . . ." Brooks then recited the events leading to the shooting. Greenshields and Leonard exchanged a few words, listening as the judge said, "Now all the court has to do is quietly and deliberately assist you in coming to the right decision." Brooks again searched through his papers, then read the charge against Morrison aloud, adding, "Now you may take this indictment as a whole, but if you think he is not quite guilty, you might find him guilty of a *lesser* crime, which does not demand the life of the prisoner. Let us take the legal aspect of the case and respective positions of Warren and the prisoner, for the prisoner, innocent or guilty, was a fugitive from justice at the time, while Warren, whether properly or not, was entrusted with a warrant and the execution thereof. . . ."

If there had been any other audible voice in the courtroom at this precise moment, it would have come from the table of the defense. Spanyaardt glanced up from his notebook to Greenshields whose body had hunched forward over the table, as though having difficulty catching Brooks's words. Leonard and Lemieux were eying each other strangely. Spanyaardt had missed the significance of what Brooks had said and quickly reread the last sentence. Then he knew what had brought the defense up short. Brooks was losing his sense of impartiality, after saying moments before "I have not the slightest wish to interfere . . ."

Judge Brooks, sensing the expectancy in the courtroom, raised his voice. "The officers of justice are under the protection of the law and for this reason the killing of officers is considered murder. All officers, whether specially appointed or not, receive the same protection. But it can only be murder if the officer is known to be properly appointed and in the discharge of his duty, otherwise the crime is simply manslaughter." Brooks paused as if letting his every word be understood, then went on: "If the prisoner at the bar knew Lucius Warren was an officer and the prisoner had been told so by Warren, the prisoner is, according to the law, guilty of murder. If he did not know this, he is guilty of manslaughter. The defense has claimed that Warren was an alien and that this deprived him of all protection, in regard to the illegality of the warrant. I will show you how it is not necessary to put all the indictments in a warrant, for this would make the carrying out of the law impossible. . . ."

Again he went through his notes then, referring to a similar case in the United States, quoted it as saying there was no excuse for killing an officer who is trying to make an arrest. This indictment in the States, said Brooks, did not contain an accurate description of the offense, but the judge held it did not matter. And regarding the alien question, where Warren was concerned, Brooks said there was *no conclusive proof* that Warren was or was not an alien. Warren was at the time of his death an officer *de facto*, and the fact that he was not legally appointed would only change the offense from murder to manslaughter. "It is for you to consider then, gentlemen," he said finally, "under the direction of the court, whether the prisoner is guilty of murder, guilty of manslaughter, or, as the defense pretend, did the act in the defense of his life." The judge's charge to the jury had ended.

It was midday. Members of the jury left their places and were escorted to a small room off to the left in the courtroom. The door was subsequently locked, with the bailiff keeping all and sundry clear. Meanwhile, Judges Brooks and Wurtele were talking quietly, while below them the clerks were busily exchanging bits of paper. Further to the left the prosecution attorney were holding a whispered conference, leaving the defense attorneys to sit, each with his own thoughts.

Peter Spanyaardt sat back, rubbing the cramps from his weary fingers. He was thinking of the judge's charge, intimating that the prisoner might be found guilty of manslaughter. The thought haunted him.

3 P.M.

Nothing had been heard from the jury. People moved about, though most remained quiet in their seats. Spanyaardt was talking to an elderly Scotsman who mentioned the portion about the manslaughter, saying, "and my heart sank within me when I heard those words, for I saw it was virtually a direction to the jury. The majority of the jury then will probably not bring him in 'not guilty.'"

4 P.M.

Though the crowd became restless, few had left.

5 P.M.

Unofficial word reached the court that a "disagreement" had delayed the jury's verdict.

5:30 P.M.

Judge Brooks adjourned the court, saying he would continue with another case, though Morrison could remain in the dock, which annoyed defense attorney Leonard who leaned over to Greenshields, saying it was contrary to usual practice not to remove the prisoner during long deliberations. Greenshields agreed. But they could do nothing, he said drily.

As time went by, speculation on the delay increased and would have continued to grow had not a "practically official" report circulated that two jurors were holding out for total acquittal while the others had taken "the judge's advice" to find for manslaughter. Morrison had finally been returned to the jail.

The lights of Sherbrooke were to burn late into the night as its citizens gathered together to discuss the case and ponder its outcome. Most of the reporters, including Peter Spanyaardt, remained to wander aimlessly about the courtroom, virtually alone, apart from the odd clerk and those guarding the door to the jury room door.

By Wednesday morning nothing had changed.

8 A.M.

The courtroom began filling with early risers, or, more likely, "all-nighters." "Some of the habitués seated even at this hour," noted a weary Spanyaardt, "look as if they had slept in that position. The old bailiff, who had caused much amusement the other day by falling asleep next to the jury box, was on watch from early this morning at the door of the jury room, preventing anyone from coming within three feet of it, as others had done through the night."

8:30 A.M.

Sherbrooke's Wellington Street and the planks of the Commercial Bridge rang with the tramping of horses, the rumble of wagons, and the footsteps of a long trail of people trudging up to the courthouse. Among the first to arrive were the counsels for the defense.

Spanyaardt found them disarmingly approachable. Taking advantage of the moment, he asked Greenshields what action would be taken should Donald Morrison be found guilty of murder. Without hesitation the lawyer commented first that he was none to happy with the judge's charge to the jury. On this basis alone, if the jury reached a "guilty" verdict, the defense would move for a reversal. On the grounds that part of the judge's charge had unduly influenced them.

Spanyaardt nodded, remembering something else. He asked if the judge hadn't omitted the usual reminder to the jury to give the prisoner the benefit of the doubt? The three lawyers glanced at Spanyaardt with due respect. It was quite so, they said. Spanyaardt thanked them and moved away, rather proud of himself.

10 A.M.

The latest of the "unofficial" reports (Spanyaardt failed to trace where these were coming from; possibly the court officials who kept the jury in food and were taking care of their other needs) had eleven jurors holding out for acquittal, one for manslaughter. It was ten-thirty. Brooks and Wurtele took their seats, allowing that the prisoner need not be brought into court for the moment.

11 A.M.

The impatience of everyone, from spectator to judge, was obvious. The reporters doodled on bits of paper, Greenshields kept turning to stare at the jury-room door and Fitzpatrick walked about in small circles. Augusta McIver had arrived alone and sat stiffly, with her hands folded in her lap.

11:20 A.M.

A loud knock broke the bored silence. All eyes swung to the

small jury-room door. The bailiff, seated stiffly before it, rose with practiced dignity, turned the key, and opened it wide enough to get his head through. He remained thus for interminable seconds.

At last the bailiff pulled back and relocked the door. High Constable Hiram Moe joined him. They exchanged covert whispers, then Moe walked solemnly to the bench for whispered conference with the judges. A clerk was dispatched to bring back the prisoner.

Donald Morrison arrived calm and seemingly unaware of the crowd as his handcuffs were removed and he stepped into the dock.

Immediately Judge Brooks ordered the court be cleared near the prisoner's dock. This done, Brooks said, "Anyone giving way to their feelings, either before or after the verdict, will be severely punished."

The room hushed.

The door to the jury room grated noisily against its hinges as it swung wide.

Camille Millette, the foreman, appeared first, looking drawn and haggard. Following him closely were the remaining eleven jurors who crowded noisily into the jury box and sat down. Millette was the only one who remained standing.

From the center of the courtroom a voice boomed, "Prisoner at the bar, arise." Morrison stood up, his face mirroring the steadiness which he had maintained since the first day of the trial.

The clerk then turned to the jury, asking, "Do you find the prisoner guilty or not guilty?"

Millette looked down at his hands and began unfolding a piece of paper sandwiched between two damp palms, then glanced up as though following stage directions in a play. Dropping his head once he read aloud, "We have agreed upon a verdict, Your Honor, and it is to the effect that the prisoner is *guilty of manslaughter*, but we hope that you will give him the *lightest* penalty which you can consciously [*sic*] give."

The courtroom was stunned into a hushed silence. In the dock the prisoner, Donald Morrison, remained as motionless as a statue.

15

THE AFTERMATH

OCTOBER 1889

Two days had passed since the jury had found Donald Morrison guilty of manslaughter, with the strongest recommendation for leniency. It was about eight o'clock Friday, October 11, and within the next two hours Morrison would appear before the judge to receive sentence.

In the two-day interim Peter Spanyaardt had found little time to himself as he worked far into Wednesday night and early Thursday morning writing the story behind the verdict. After very little sleep, he had gone out Thursday to interview as many people as possible connected with the case and spent many hours seeking permission to talk with the prisoner Donald Morrison. He was told final authority could come only from Attorney General Turcotte in Quebec and he had fired off several telegrams trying to track the man down. In the meantime he heard that defense lawyer Greenshields, upset over the verdict, had asked for a deferred sentence until the defense could raise objections to the trial. His request had not been granted. The Crown had been agreed, however, that should Morrison be found guilty, all other charges pertaining to the case would be dropped, including those against people accused of aiding and abetting Morrison while evading the law.

Thursday afternoon Spanyaardt, through a stroke of good

luck, had been awaiting Turcotte's word about a possible interview when he chanced to pass the sheriff's office in the courthouse and found a long line of witnesses and jurors waiting for reimbursement for their time and travel. Among them were jury foreman Camille Millette and juror John Noyes. Realizing he had nothing to lose, Spanyaardt asked them about the trial's outcome. At first both refused to talk. The reporter mentioned that a rumor had gone around the courtroom while the jurors were deliberating that they had been divided on the verdict.

Noyes took immediate exception. "We *never* entertained a verdict of murder," he said indignantly. "We took a vote on that as soon as we came out of court and no one was in favor of it. The reason it took us so long to decide was that we wanted to go carefully over the evidence."

Millette agreed. "The arguments on either side had not the least effect on us nor the charge of the judge. The evidence was the only thing we considered." At this moment a long-faced, nervous clerk stepped from the sheriff's office. His department had run out of ready cash, he announced apologetically, and those still unpaid would have to return the next day. Millette and Noyes were not impressed, but, as Millette reasoned, they would at least be around to hear the sentence.

Later on Thursday Peter Spanyaardt returned to the clerk's office, asking if word had arrived from Attorney General Turcotte. The young, abrupt woman at the counter nodded. It had, she said. Well then? he asked. It had been rejected. Spanyaardt suddenly felt that both Noyes and Millette were kindred spirits; bureaucracy was at times rather difficult to take.

Friday morning, before the court resumed for the issuing of the sentence, J. N. Greenshields and François Lemieux stopped at the prison to visit their client. As they were ushered into his cell, Morrison broke down. "I weep," he said forlornly, "because I have to lose you, not because I fear my punishment. You have done all that human beings could do to save me, and whatever sentence the judge may impose I will accept it . . . I will serve my term uncomplainingly and, if God spares me, will return to my home perhaps a better and wiser man."

Both Greenshields and Lemieux remained motionless, touched deeply. Morrison then reached down and picked up two

THE AFTERMATH 213

canes from the floor and handing one to each said, "I am sorry I can do nothing on my own to repay you for your labor, but while I was in the woods I made two canes. Accept them please and believe in my everlasting gratitude."

The lawyers looked down at the canes in their hands. They were of black thorny wood with crooked handles. For a full minute no one spoke. Then solemnly the lawyers shook hands with Morrison and walked from the cell. Greenshields stopped beyond the bars and looked back. In the corner sat Remi Lamontagne, a hardened criminal who, unashamedly moved by the scene, ignored the tears rolling down his own cheeks. Greenshields turned away, putting a hand up to his face.

The courtroom was jam-packed when Peter Spanyaardt made his way through the crowd and reached the other reporters. He had only now learned that the jurors had each signed a petition asking Judge Brooks to give the mildest sentence possible, reinforcing their recommendation for leniency. This petition had been signed when they realized they had gone too far with their verdict.

Now the final disposition of the case rested entirely on Judge Brooks.

At precisely ten o'clock Judges Brooks and Wurtele took their places. With the formalities dispensed with and the prisoner told to remain standing, Brooks said loudly, "Donald Morrison, have you anything to say why sentence should not be passed upon you?"

"No, sir," Donald answered steadily, "I have not."

Brooks cleared his throat and glanced down at his notes, then began reading. "Donald Morrison, you have been, after a fair and impartial trial, before a jury of your own peers, after an able defense in which your interests have been protected by the most able counsel, convicted of the crime of manslaughter. You were indicted for the crime of murder. The difference between the two is so slight that it was exceedingly fortunate for you that the court is not now called upon to pass the sentence of death, instead of a term of imprisonment. The jury before whom you were tried have found, instead of murder, that you are guilty of the crime of manslaughter."

Brooks paused, took a sip of water, and continued without looking up. "The jury, in their verdict, have recommended you to the mercy of the court. They have asked that the slightest penalty consistent with the requirements of law . . . should be passed upon you. These recommendations always receive the fullest attention on behalf of the court . . ."

Across the courtroom Spanyaardt was hurriedly taking down every word, only to be momentarily distracted by the growing anxiety which was not confined to the crowd alone, but shared among the counsels, jurors, and clerks alike.

"The court cannot, however, be ignorant of this fact, of which they have official cognizance: after you had willingly and feloniously killed and slain one Lucius Warren, on the 22 June 1888, you did not submit yourself to the authorities. Now the amount of punishment to be inflicted upon you has been the subject of the most anxious and careful consideration of this court. The punishment is not against the individual, it is not inflicted . . . for the purpose of punishing him only, but for the protection of society and feeling the responsibility which is placed upon it, the court feels you must be sentenced to a long term of imprisonment . . ."

A gasp echoed about the bare walls of the courtroom.

"With the view of impressing this fact on the public mind, it is the duty of this court to impose upon you a sentence which shall mark the enormity and gravity of the crime you have been convicted of. But, Donald Morrison"—the words came slow and deliberate—"up to the time of your capture you evidently had not repented of the crime you had committed. You are still a young man. . . ."

Everyone in the courtroom, save the judge himself, was balanced on the edge of his seat, as yet not fully aware of the gravity of Brooks's words: "long term of imprisonment," "enormity of the crime," "not repented." Surely he was being a little hard on the prisoner . . . !

"By diligence, industry, and faithfulness and strict observance of the prison rules . . . for the first six months, it is possible to deduct five days a month, for subsequent months . . ."

Then quite unexpectedly came the sentence, couched within the same dreary monotone: ". . . and the sentence that the court pronounces is that you be confined in the provincial penitentiary at St. Vincent de Paul at hard labor for the term of eighteen years."

A deadly hush fell.

Jailer Reed waited the appropriate two or three seconds, then methodically reached back for the door of the prisoner's dock. Moments flitted by as the clicking sounds of the handcuffs snapping into place sprang across the room to echo against the wall. Before anyone realized, Donald Morrison and his five stern guards were moving up the center aisle of the courtroom.

It was Camille Millette whose rasping voice finally broke the utter silence. "Good God," he exclaimed, "we never expected that. . . ."

But it was too late.

Suddenly the crowd came to life. As if given a signal, it surged forward, enveloping the guards and their prisoner as the small procession stepped through the hallway and out onto the portico where Morrison, quite without expression, stopped to look about him, his eyes searching the crowd.

Behind him Peter Spanyaardt leaned heavily against one of the large concrete pillars, watching the drama finally come to an end.

They had reached the sidewalk now, the crowd and the guards flanking the prisoner. Peter Spanyaardt had seen enough, and as he turned away his eye caught sight of a young woman half buried in the crush who was frantically fighting her way forward. He watched as at last she broke free and, stumbling forward, quite suddenly hurled herself between two unsuspecting guards and wrapped her arms tightly around the prisoner as his long arms encircled her.

And from where he stood, Spanyaardt believed it to be the woman called Augusta McIver.

EPILOGUE

At one o'clock on Tuesday afternoon, June 19, 1894, a broken, dying man of thirty-six years was brought hurriedly into the emergency ward of the Royal Victoria Hospital in Montreal. An initial examination showed he had a temperature of 101 degrees Fahrenheit, his pulse was a quick 150, and his respiratory rate a fast 42. Doctors diagnosed his sickness as phthisis, better known as pulmonary consumption, or "wasting disease." The patient was registered under file number 69. His name was listed as Donald Morrison.

Donald Morrison had spent more than four and a half years in St. Vincent de Paul Penitentiary, located north of the island of Montreal, managing only to survive the first eighteen months without incident. It was then that he suddenly refused to eat. Not knowing exactly how to handle such a case, prison officials watched helplessly as the prisoner grew progressively weaker. When at last he became too weak to resist, food was forced into him.

However, if the authorities won this round, they lost the next: Donald began starving himself mentally and emotionally. Against this the authorities were powerless. Existence for Morrison had died with his sentencing on October 11, 1889.

For the next three years prisoner number 2329 was listless,

morose, and took no active part in prison life. Slowly his tall, handsome figure became the tired, bent one of an old man.

Word of his worsening condition finally reached his friends and relatives. Police who once hunted him, lawyers who once prosecuted him, newspapermen who once befriended him, all tried in vain to show him life still had meaning. It was to no avail. Born to the freedom of the open country, Donald Morrison could not survive in captivity.

It was the prison's chaplain, Canon Fulton, who first noticed that Morrison was *seriously* ill. Though Dr. Godette, the physician, kept a close eye on the prisoner, Donald went slowly about his duties without sign of pain, without complaint. At last, however, the clergyman was allowed to bring in an outside specialist, Dr. Stewart, of the Royal Victoria, who prescribed certain medicines for him. His time was wasted; Morrison refused to take them.

This was the stubborn Donald Morrison of old, who had refused to let his sentence be reviewed or appealed. This was the stubborn Morrison who now, inches from death, refused to save his own life, while his friends and admirers stood helplessly by wondering what could possibly restore the broken man.

Malcolm Matheson, Hugh Leonard, and others found the only way. The old Morrison Defense Organization was given new life as it launched a campaign to lobby and plead with Ottawa and the federal government of Canada to give the dying man one last chance for survival by letting him spend what was left of his life back in his beloved Megantic country.

His friends worked hard, writing letters, contacting anyone they thought might help to grant Donald a pardon. And when the situation looked the bleakest, news suddenly reached Montreal and the Eastern Townships that Minister of Justice Sir John Thompson in Ottawa had signed the recommendation granting Donald Morrison his release. It was Saturday, June 16, 1894.

Peter Spanyaardt was in the editorial office of the *Star* on St. James Street in Montreal when he heard the news. Without waiting to pick up his hat, coat, pen, or notebook, he rushed down the stairs and out onto the street, heading for the penitentiary beyond the backwaters of Rivière des Prairies.

Within two hours Deputy Warden McCarthy stood beside Morrison's cot, saying, "I have just received news, Donald, which gives me hope that the order for your release will be here within the next three or four days. . . ."

The utter frustration of having to wait *three or four days* while a man's life was counted off in minutes completely baffled the Defense Organization and Morrison's many friends. Nothing, they found, could process the pardon any faster.

Then shortly before noon on Tuesday, June 19, the order of release reached the deputy warden. Outside a carriage waited.

Donald Morrison appeared, wearing an old dark suit. Supporting him on either side were Canon Fulton and Peter Spanyaardt, as the Megantic Outlaw took his first step to freedom. He brought with him his worldly wealth: $10 given each released prisoner, a dollar sent by an old lady, and a penny of his own.

Donald was made comfortable in the clergyman's carriage. He looked up at Fulton, but didn't have the strength to ask where they were going.

Dr. Stewart and his medical staff were waiting for the carriage to arrive at the emergency entrance of the Royal Victoria Hospital. After a hurried examination, Donald was given whiskey, milk and one thirtieth of a gram of strychnine. They hoped it might help.

But it came too late. Donald Morrison died shortly before 4 P.M., Tuesday, June 19, 1894.

At seven-thirty Wednesday night a funeral service was held in the operating room at the "Royal Vic"; the rosewood casket bearing Donald Morrison's body was then carried down through the city to the railway station, accompanied by more than two hundred of his friends and admirers. It was placed aboard the Canadian Pacific Railway's Montreal–Halifax train, and at four o'clock the next morning the body arrived at the Marsden station where, five years before almost to the hour, a wounded Donald Morrison had lain bound in blankets and rugs as he waited for the special train to take him into captivity.

Burial took place in the Guisla Cemetery, just down the road from where Sophia and Murdo Morrison lived out their years and a quarter of a mile from where the police had waited in ambush, ready to capture him dead or alive, during an agreed truce.

As for the police, each of those personally involved in the capture of the Megantic Outlaw received some reward. Constable McMahon became a sergeant a day or two following the ambush. Montreal Police Chief Hughes got his policemen back before Montreal citizens became too annoyed; he also gave Sergeant McMahon a new Colt, in a trade for the one McMahon had taken from Morrison.

As for Leroyer, he probably got a portion of the monetary reward, though not as much, perhaps, as he had hoped. Quebec Premier Mercier was later to announce: "I cannot say how it [the reward] will be paid. I do not know if any time was specified in the proclamation." Chief Hughes felt that "the $3,000 should be shared among *all* who took part in the capture."

Exhaustive research leaves little doubt that the truce leading to Morrison's capture had been violated or, more accurately in the words of Major McMinn at the time of the capture, "We have been deceived, and Morrison has been betrayed during a pretended truce." It was all too convenient that "those in charge" had left for the weekend. Judge Dugas had been under a great deal of pressure from the government to settle the matter with Morrison, but no one knows who the originator was of the betrayal scheme.

And the fires and rifle shots at Auguste Duquette's farm, which led to the shooting of Lucius "Jack" Warren? The facts about those have never been unearthed. It was not likely the work of Donald Morrison, who had been with others on two of the three occasions.

As for Augusta McIver, she later returned permanently to Boston, Massachusetts, to marry. Peter Spanyaardt never did meet her. He eventually forsook the news and rewrite desks to become sports editor of the Montreal *Star*.

One curious footnote remains. Donald's small headstone, still intact in the Guisla Cemetery, displays a mysterious mistake. It correctly bears his birth date, March 15, 1858, but it states his death was June 25, 1889.

Many theories have been postulated about the latter date. Friends say it marked his capture, "the day he really died." However his capture was on Easter Sunday, April 21, 1889.

But maybe Donald Morrison's friends are in fact *closer* to the truth. He *really* died moments after saying good-by to his parents as he turned to step from the log house that Easter Sunday evening, at nine o'clock.

ACKNOWLEDGMENTS

My thanks to all those who helped bring this story to life, particularly Mr. and Mrs. Duncan McLeod of Milan (known formerly as the village of Marsden), Quebec; Marie Jeanne Daigneau, of Sherbrooke, Quebec, who keeps the Eastern Townships Historical Board going strong; Norah Leonard of Sherbrooke, daughter of the late John Leonard, Donald Morrison's friend and legal counsel; Mary Morrison of Montreal, who was one of many to serve Donald Morrison meals during "the hunt"; Max Lapointe, retired head of the Montreal *Star* library, and the library staff; historian J. Alex Edmison, Q.C., of Ottawa; Carol Tuck of Canada Wide Services; and Theresa Butcher, Montreal *Star* library.